Mosaics of Redemption

DISCOVERING GOD'S RESTORATION IN
OUR BROKEN AND SHATTERED LIVES

Barry K. Gaeddert

Permission

For Zachary and Micah. Any time I miss your mother, I look at you and see her smile, hear her laugh, and recognize her loving heart. You inspire me. Thank you for loving me so bravely.

I GRATEFULLY ACKNOWLEDGE the countless people who loved us, walked with us, and prayed with and for us throughout our entire journey and beyond.

I am especially thankful for John, Glen, Matt, Will, and Tom (and others too numerous to mention), for listening patiently to my rantings and ravings as well as to my rebellion and cursing. You allowed me to weep tears upon tears. And you loved me through the darkest, most frightening, most painful days of my life.

A special thank-you to Jack, Annie, Cory, and Sarah, for reading this manuscript and giving input and feedback to me. Your insights and advice helped to shape it and make it something worthwhile.

And with tears of joy and gratitude, I want to express my profound love for Zachary and Micah, Ted and Anne, Mom and Dad, and the rest of the family, all of whom also suffered from this devastating loss yet will forever know the joy of being loved deeply by Suzy. God is still revealing his redemptive mosaics in our lives.

Preface

I DIDN'T WANT to write a book.

I didn't want to write *this* book.

For all of the lessons learned, insights gained, character changes, and maturing outlook on life that I have experienced, I would prefer an alternative. There is not a day that goes by that I would not trade the wisdom attained or the changes in my character just to have my wife, Suzy, back. My whole being aches and longs to have her here with me. I would give up any gain or growth if it meant I could hold her hand again.

But I can't do that.

So instead I share with you the lessons God taught me through our journey. Some people will think I am crazy to say that God spoke to me. I hope that you will bear with me because it has been through the fire of our trial—Suzy's diagnosis, treatments, decline, and death and my grief after her death—that God has profoundly spoken with me. I share those messages with you in this book.

In my previous book, *The Shattered Vase*, I shared the story of our journey *as it happened*. I wrote a blog throughout the four years of our trudge in and through the messiness of brain cancer. Those blog entries are presented chronologically, without changes or narration, in *The Shattered Vase*.

In this book I choose to narrate. I choose to translate. I choose to explain, describe, and help you know what God has revealed to me. I am not sure I have any mature insights or wisdom of my own. But I humbly offer to you that which God has shared with me. I have built upon the previous book to help narrate our story in this book and to illustrate the beautiful new designs that I believe God is making in the brokenness of my life. You will find a few of my blog entries scattered among the chapters. The stories in the pages that follow hopefully illustrate tangible examples of God's redeeming work in our lives, even when everything had fallen and was broken all around us.

I have not written a memorial tribute to Suzy. I would love to do that. But that is not the purpose or intention of this book. I recognize that I have a very high need to talk about Suzy. One thing that I have learned in talking with others who grieve is that our need to talk is much higher than most people's ability to listen. So lending your patient ear and compassionate time to a grieving brother or sister is a great gift indeed.

Instead this book is written to share my reflections on the journey through Suzy's illness from diagnosis through two brain surgeries, treatment, recurrences, her palliative (end-of-life) care, decline, and death. It ventures then into my own life after her death and the wonderings and wanderings of trying to make sense of it all.

Where was God? Where is God? What possible purpose could there be in this? If God can heal, why doesn't he? If God is holy, why doesn't he show that? If God is loving, why does he allow this? Why do I feel so alone? Why do our sons have to live the rest of their lives without their mother's physical presence and tangible love? What on earth could ever come from this hellish journey? What in heaven could be going on when I am in so much pain?

You shouldn't expect there to be a lot of answers, at least not any short, pat answers. This will not all get tied up with a nice pretty bow. You will not reach the end of this book and then nod and smile as you go on with your life. I admit that I still struggle with some of this. Perhaps I always will. The new designs that God is creating in my life are still in process, so this story does not have the feel of being finished or completed. There are still moments when I am confused, frustrated, and even angry. I still have questions. But there are some thoughts, some themes, some recurring pieces of the journey, and I think it is good to share those with you.

I believe that God is picking up the broken pieces of our lives and creating something new, a new mosaic that reflects his redemptive work in our lives. Consider the following insight:

> *When suffering shatters the carefully kept vase that is our lives, God stoops to pick up the pieces. But he doesn't put them back together as a restoration project patterned after our former selves. Instead, He sifts through the rubble and selects some of the shards as raw material for another project—a mosaic that tells the story of redemption.*

> —*Ken Gire*, Windows of the Soul

Because of a brain tumor that led to my wife's death, I see a portion of my life as a shattered vase. I have certainly known and experienced brokenness and an upside-down time in my walk on earth. Our lives were uprooted, turned over, turned inside out, and, indeed, turned upside down. It has been painful. It has been lonely. It is a journey I never wanted. It is a life of which I never dreamed.

Yet in spite of it all, these affirmations remain true: God is trustworthy in spite of the script. God is present in spite of seeming distant. God is holy in spite of the brokenness. God is loving in spite of the pain. Those statements are all so very upside down and backward. They are the premise of this book, the foundational truths that I believe God showed me on this journey.

Each of us experiences pain and brokenness in varying ways and on diverse levels. Some are dealing with a painful past, while others struggle to face an uncertain or pain-filled future. Many are dealing with both. I pray that you can begin to see and know the mosaics of redemption that God brought in my life. These new mosaics were created from the broken shards of the shattered vase. Together we can discover new insights, wisdom, and maturity that God offers to each of us in the pain and brokenness of our own shattered lives.

The Background Story

I BEGAN MY studies at Fuller Theological Seminary on a bright, sunny day in September 1985. Gathering all of the wisdom and lessons learned in the twenty-three years of my life, I was ready to follow the calling that I believed God had placed on my life. I was eager and enthusiastic to pursue a degree that would lead to ordination and a career as a full-time ordained pastor.

As I walked to the building in which my very first class was held, I met a young woman with an enormous smile. We exchanged greetings, and as we talked, we realized that we were both not only starting our seminary studies at the same time but also headed to the same first class. I opened the door for her. We walked up two flights of stairs and entered the classroom. I sat down next to her. My life was forever changed from that encounter.

Everything about this woman, Suzy, appealed to me. She was enthusiastically extroverted. Her smile lit up the room. She chatted comfortably with people from various backgrounds, ethnicities, and experiences. Suzy was carefree and full of life. She loved Jesus and wanted to serve him with all of her heart. And she had an uncanny ability to make every single person she encountered feel as if he or she was the most important person in all the world. Undoubtedly, I was in love!

We came from drastically different backgrounds. I grew up in a small town in Kansas. Family vacations most often entailed a two-hour car ride to visit our grandparents on the farm. I had graduated from high school knowing almost every person in my class. Suzy, on the other hand, had grown up in Saudi Arabia, where her parents worked for an oil company. She had traveled the world, visiting the Louvre in Paris, France, and the Hermitage in St. Petersburg, Russia. Her family once vacationed on a safari in Africa. She met and became friends with classmates and acquaintances across the globe.

Suzy and I formed a quick and lasting friendship. We spent large amounts of time together, sometimes studying, sometimes walking on the beach, often eating, and always talking, laughing, and sharing life. It became very clear that God had called us to share our lives and ministries together. We were married on December 12, 1987.

We served in church and campus ministries in central Kansas; St. Louis, Missouri; and London, England. Suzy became known as an expert on evangelism and small groups. I developed skills in Bible teaching and preaching. We often counseled or shared our lives with guests in our home, usually over an exquisite meal that Suzy had prepared. She was also an outstanding cook.

God blessed us with two sons, Zachary and Micah. Both were excellent students and gifted athletes. Our family loved to travel and to serve in short-term mission experiences together. We led teams from our church to help build houses in Tijuana, Mexico, and to care for orphans in the Vologda Oblast of Russia. We loved and served God with the very best energy and commitment that we could offer.

Our lives changed suddenly and drastically in 2010 when Suzy was diagnosed with a malignant and highly aggressive form of brain cancer. Our sons were sixteen and thirteen on the day we had to tell them this news. Their lives were forever changed as well. Given a prognosis of fifteen to eighteen months, Suzy chose to live with as much passion for Jesus as she possibly could. Knowing that her time on earth was short, she wholeheartedly continued doing what she had always been passionate about: telling others that they matter to God and that he loves them and wants to live in relationship with them.

Suzy lived for three and a half years after her diagnosis. In the final months, the tumor cruelly assaulted her body, depriving her of cognitive function and even changing her personality. She lost the ability to walk and eventually lost the ability to speak. Suzy graciously and courageously walked through every phase of her brain-tumor journey. Finally, on September 17, 2013, just a few months short of our twenty-sixth wedding anniversary, Jesus called his precious daughter home.

Our story—from diagnosis through treatment and recurrence to Suzy's decline and death, as well as my journey through grief after her death—is recorded in this book. My deep prayer is that the lessons God taught, the perspectives God shared, and the insights God offered to me can also encourage you. Whether your journey is dark and frightening or filled with hope, my longing is that you will be encouraged to consider the redemptive mosaics God wants to create from any broken and shattered parts of your own life.

As the best cheerleader I could imagine, Suzy would have cheered me on in this writing project. She would have cheered for you also, dear reader, and wanted you to know how precious you are to the God who created you. She would have patiently answered your questions and prayed with and for you as you struggle through your own journey. She would have loved you.

And I am quite certain that you would have loved her as well.

An Upside-Down World

"All the World's Turned Upside Down"

If buttercups buzzed after the bee,
If boats were on land, churches on sea,
If ponies rode men, and if grass ate the cows,
And if cats should be chased into holes by the mouse,
If summer were spring, and the other way 'round,
Then all the world would be upside down.
Derry down, down, hey derry down,
Then all the world would be upside down.

—Traditional English ballad

Chapter 1

God Is Trustworthy in Spite of the Script

Diagnosis, brain surgery, and treatment: 2010

On February 8, 2010, my wife, Suzy, was diagnosed with a brain tumor. She had been struggling with some health issues for several weeks. As I look back, she had not been well for a few months. She couldn't remember simple things. She sometimes repeated herself or needed me to repeat things several times before she understood them. Finally, after Suzy woke up with a headache each morning for many days, we went to the hospital emergency room.

The doctor ran several diagnostic tests. She put Suzy through a battery of questions and procedures that I came to be all too familiar with over the next three and a half years. The doctor ordered a CAT scan. We were then escorted into a private room and told to wait for the doctor. Suzy told me that after the first scan, the technician came in and told her that they were going to inject dye into her veins and do another scan. This was not part of the original plan. We both knew something was not right.

The doctor arrived. She was clearly uncomfortable. She made some small talk. Then she looked at Suzy and said, "You have a tumor in your brain." The words still echo in my head as clearly (and painfully) as they did in those first terrifying minutes after they were uttered.

Suzy's first brain surgery was scheduled within two weeks. Following that surgery, we learned the results of the pathology report: glioblastoma multiform, grade 4, or GBM for short. This is a highly malignant and extremely aggressive form of cancer. Statistics tell us that it is 100 percent fatal (although there are certainly some who are living with GBM and defying that diagnosis!). A normal life expectancy at first diagnosis is fifteen to eighteen months.

Following surgery, Suzy began a six-week regimen of radiation therapy combined with oral chemotherapy. The plan was to then follow this with another six months of chemotherapy at increasingly higher amounts. Suzy was only able to tolerate four of those chemotherapy doses before the decision was made to discontinue the treatments, thus ending the initial treatment phase for Suzy's brain tumor.

The Script
The stories of our lives unfold like the script of a movie. Some stories are romantic, others comedic. Drama fills many scripts. There are action, adventure, and mystery interwoven in them. Sadly, some scripts contain horrific scenes as painful and chilling events unfold, most often without our ability to change or impact the story in any way.

I do not like the script of our story.

I would write a different script. I would immediately write a script in which Suzy did not have a brain tumor. In fact, if I could, I would write a script where no person in the world has a tumor. Or any kind of cancer. Or any disease. If I couldn't change that, I certainly would have changed the way that Suzy's brain surgery and radiation treatments affected her, causing her pain and memory loss. I did not like that part of the script.

As the disease progressed, there were additional challenges and difficulties (as you will read in later chapters). I would have changed all of that as well if I could rewrite the script. I would certainly write a different ending to this story. I would eliminate the horror scenes. Who should ever have to face the decision to end medical treatment for your spouse's (or your own) illness? Even though Suzy's death was inevitable, she lingered so long in the final days, struggling with horrendous pain, deeply confused by what was happening to her and around her.

What is the scriptwriter doing? What message is he giving? Where is God's presence in this horror-filled script? Can we trust that what he is writing is good? This is not to my liking.

I would write a different script.

The Wilderness

Suzy's diagnosis and treatments thrust us into a world for which we were ill-prepared. We had no previous life experience that we could use to help make sense of the new journey had begun. How should one react, and what actions should one take if faced with tragedy? One might be able to imagine what one will do or wonder what one will say. But one can never actually *know* until that moment.

Soon after we learned the news that Suzy's tumor was grade 4, I remember wishing to be in a different place than where we found ourselves. I longed for the possibility to change the script. I found myself identifying with the Israelites wandering in the desert. They had left behind a land and life that were familiar. No matter how much they longed for it, they were never going back to Egypt. But they were not yet to the Promised Land. There was a bright and hope-filled future. But they were not yet there. And that is how I felt. When the news of the diagnosis came, we quickly realized that we had left behind a life to which we would never, ever return, no matter how great our longing. God was gently leading us to a new land, but we were not yet there. We were living in the in-between time, the in-between place. We were in the wilderness. And I wanted to change the script to get us out of there.

If I were one of those Israelites, I'm not sure I would have done very well. I don't like camping. In fact I hate it. I would have said to God, "You want me to follow a pillar of cloud each day and fire each night? Yeah, right. Where can I buy a map?" The Bible tells us that God provided manna each day for them to eat but that those who gathered more than a day's supply found it rotten the next morning. I am sure that it would have taken me a long time to stop secretly trying to stash away a little extra. I like to plan. I like to know the agenda. I like to manage a systematic program, lining up the supplies and getting everything in order. Trusting God to guide only enough for one day and provide only enough for one day would have been quite challenging for someone like me.

Yet the wilderness was exactly where God had placed us. He only provided enough guidance for one day, although he provided abundant manna each day. And he wanted me to trust him to keep walking, keep journeying, keep trusting each day. My struggles with the challenge of doing this became a painful insight into my character.

Over time I was forced to learn that I needed to hold things very loosely while wandering in the wilderness. There were a thousand and one decisions to make, and we didn't have enough information to make any of them. It felt lonely and confusing when I wanted to have control and every ounce of control was taken away from me. I wanted to go back to Egypt! I wanted to get to the Promised Land! Anything, please, Lord, but just not here in the wilderness!

"Follow the pillar; it will guide your next step. Collect the manna; there will be enough to meet your needs today. The decision will be made when it needs to be made. Until then: trust. Just trust. Just walk humbly and faithfully, trusting that I see what you cannot see and know what you do not yet know."

The tears continued to flow, many times each day. But I started to see our family being held and carried in hands bigger and stronger and more loving than any we had ever known before this point in our lives. And that was a good, good, good place to be. It was very upside down. It took time to embrace and accept it, but it became a place of solace and comfort once I learned to trust God as the script of our lives unfolded.

Superpowers

After Suzy's brain surgery, she began a long regimen of radiation therapy combined with chemotherapy. This also turned our lives upside down. It was as if boats were on land and cats were being chased into holes by mice. And I didn't like it. Again, I wanted a different script. Again, I begged the scriptwriter to change the story, to rearrange the events, to write a different storyline than the upside-down one in which we were living. Yet the scriptwriter remained silent.

As I watched Suzy deal with the fatigue, nausea, and loss of patches of hair that her treatment caused, I often longed to change the script instantaneously. I wanted to be able to snap my fingers and make it all go away. I used to think that if I were a superhero, I would want my superpower to be that I could become invisible. I never wanted to be able to fly. That is so impractical. Being invisible seemed more useful. But as our script unfolded, I realized that I would prefer a superpower that allowed me to snap my fingers and change a situation. It sure would have been handy. Snapping my fingers seemed a far simpler solution than dealing with the daily grind of medicines, all given at specific times, and long daily trips to the hospital for the radiation treatments. Snapping my fingers to remove the challenges, the barriers, the frustrations, the heartache—what an easy solution that would have made everyone happy.

Sadly, I will never be a superhero. When I was younger, I used to love to watch *Bewitched*. I can wiggle my nose like Samantha but without the same results. So I have to approach life without these superpowers and learn to make do with what I have.

There are two truths that I focused on that gave great encouragement to a superpowerless guy like me:

1) God is sovereign. That means that he is in *control*; he has the *authority* to work it all out. If God were 90 percent

sovereign, then, by definition, he would not be sovereign. It is a 100 percent thing. And that gives me great comfort. I may not understand his ways or agree with his plan. I don't have to. I rest confidently knowing that he is sovereign, the one reigning and ruling over all of life. Especially since I don't have superpowers, this truth strengthens me.

2) In our pain, in our grief and loss, in our brokenness, we must remember that *it will not always be like this*. We may not be able to snap our fingers to make it go away. But make no mistake: one day it will go away. And the assurance of that promise brings me peace. It reminds me when I am at my lowest that the way things are now is only temporary. Something far better, far greater, will replace it. Something that will then go on forever and ever.

And I heard a loud voice from the throne saying,
"Look! God's dwelling place is now among the people,
and he will dwell with them.
They will be his people, and God himself will be with them
and be their God.
He will wipe every tear from their eyes.
There will be no more death or mourning or crying or pain,
for the old order of things has passed away."

—*Revelation 21:3–5*

Unquestionably there were days when I wanted God to snap his fingers and make the whole "old order of things" pass away. In the script that I longed to write, I wanted this to happen immediately. But until the old order does pass away, I will wait in trusting, eager anticipation. I'm not a superhero; that is for sure. But I am content to just be God's child and let him hold me. I am grateful that will never change.

Given the chance, I would write a different script. I would write one with a happy ending. In my script, all the bad things would be pushed away. I'm not sure how the script would unfold. But it would definitely not have been *this* script.

But I am not God. I don't have that ability or power.

And you don't want me to be God. I am narrow-minded, self-absorbed, and immature. I am sinful. I might be able to write a script that fits what I want. But I could never be God and write a script that you want.

So the questions remain: Can we trust God even when we don't see how he is working in our lives? Can we trust that God is still good in spite of the script he is authoring?

You may be facing a difficult medical diagnosis. You may be grieving the loss of a dear friend or loved one. Your heart may ache because of the rebellion of your child. Perhaps you were told that you were no longer valuable to your employer and asked to pack up the items in your desk. Maybe your spouse has told you that he or she no longer wants to pursue the holy relationship to which you feel God has called you. Each of us, all of us, at some time, in some way, longs to have a different script for the drama of our lives.

Trusting God when life takes you down a dark alley is an enormous challenge. It is a blind walk—as if you are stepping out onto a precipice with deep canyons all around you into which you might fall. Trust is frightening; it is disconcerting. Oh, to be able to take the pen and write a different script!

Yet trust is the path offered by a wise, all-knowing, all-powerful God. Not answers. Not magic formulas. Just trust. Hand-in-hand, arm-in-arm trust. In and through and in spite of the dark and broken path of our present upside-down script.

When our lives are turned upside down, can we rely on God's trustworthiness in spite of the script?

CHAPTER 2

God Is Present in Spite of Seeming Distant

A period without treatment or tumor progression: 2011–12

AFTER SUZY'S DIAGNOSIS and during her first year of treatment, I was often reminded of God's promise to Jacob in Genesis 28:15, "I am with you and will watch over you wherever you go." Throughout the journey of that first year, the one thing (perhaps the only thing) that was constant was God's presence. Sometimes he was quietly present, and sometimes he was overwhelmingly present. Sometimes he was stunningly present. Sometimes he was surprisingly present. Always he was graciously, lovingly, abundantly present.

At times on the journey the sun shone brightly. There were experiences of serene confidence and joy in the beauty of each moment. At other times the wind howled and the waves crashed hard. The torrents of dark loneliness seemed to edge out any thought or hope of God's presence. Still, there he was. Faithfully. Unswervingly. Present. Always.

In the world of GBM, a year is a long, long time. I acknowledge that every single day we were given was a gift of life and breath. Not for one second do I take that for granted. I cherished the gift God had given to us in that first year. As I looked ahead, I wondered how many more days, how many more years, Suzy and I would have together.

No matter how uncertain the future, one thing of which I remained certain was that God would always be with us. No matter the circumstances. Regardless of sunshine or storm, joy or pain. I remained confident that God would go with us. And he did.

Because of my experience, I am convinced more than ever that God always will go with all of us. He will carry us when we are weak and nudge us when we are complacent. He will encourage us when we are down and celebrate with us when we are happy. But always, always, in every step—present. With us. There are many things I don't know, but this is one thing I have learned and can acknowledge with absolute certainty.

The psalmist also looked at the storms and struggles, the joys and celebrations. And he, too, acknowledged God's presence in it all:

God is our refuge and strength, an ever present help in trouble.
Therefore we will not fear, though the earth give way
and the mountains fall into the heart of the sea,
though its waters roar and foam
and the mountains quake with their surging…The Lord Almighty
is with us;
the God of Jacob is our fortress.

—Psalm 46:1–3, 7

There are many things we want. But there is only one thing we need. And the one thing we need is the one thing God gives: his presence. God is with us. Always.

Yet sometimes we still feel as if God is not present. Sometimes we can feel abandoned or alone. The circumstances of our situations may cause us to question God's presence and doubt that he is walking alongside us. Our feelings begin to take over. They run away with our hearts, and we wonder if God could possibly be present if we do not see or experience him. How can we know, really know, that God is present in those times when it feels as if he is distant and removed from us?

After eight months of treatment, Suzy swallowed her last chemotherapy medicine. It was the end of the treatment phase for her brain tumor. Of course, we didn't know it at the time. She was scheduled for two more chemo bursts in the coming months. Her blood counts were plummeting, however, after each burst. We eventually decided to cancel those final two bursts.

For almost eighteen months after the end of the treatment, Suzy remained tumor-free. We encountered a time of fewer visits to the doctors, occasional scans and blood tests, and relatively few complications. There were, however, residual effects from the damage done by the tumor before the surgery as well as the effects of radiation on her brain. Even though we had a reprieve from the cancer, our lives were not normal, and there were still daily struggles and challenges as we learned to live, temporarily, in this new place in which God had placed us. And in that tumor-free time, there was always a cloud hovering on the not-too-distant horizon. We knew that GBM would one day return. It is an excruciating challenge to try to live a joy-filled existence when every headache, every forgotten word, or every distant stare might be the signal telling us that the tumor was back.

These distractions, even while things were seemingly going well, often caused me to wonder if God was still present and walking with us as I had so intensely experienced during the treatment phase. My feelings fluctuated wildly; sometimes I felt supremely confident that God was there with us, and other times I wondered if he was anywhere near at all. I looked for ways to know and experience God's profound and unquestionable presence in the days when it sometimes felt as if he were nowhere to be found.

Christian Community at Its Best (and Worst)

One of the amazing ways that God meets us and cares for us in the challenges of our faith is through the community that surrounds us. Our churches, our small groups, our neighbors, and our lifelong friends all become critically important in new ways when we walk through the painful valleys of this life. Although God is invisible, he is still knowable. And in spite of seeming distant, he is still very present with us. He shows this in many ways, but it is often most significantly experienced in our relationships with others. *It is here, in community, that the invisible and distant God most often becomes visible and tangible.*

One of the healing communities I experienced was a group of others who also struggled with brain tumors. These brave warriors and their caregivers were life preservers in the deep sea where we found ourselves drowning. In my grief after Suzy's death, my closest friends and confidants were others who had also lost a spouse. This group was a community of healing and comfort for me. They became not only a significant source of needed information but, more importantly, were the listening ears when I needed to talk. They knew from their own journeys not to give advice. Instead, they listened, loved, and said, "Yes, I understand." That meant the world to me.

It was, however, the Christian community that carried the vast weight of our burden. Our local congregation, along with brothers and sisters all over the world, became the hands and feet of Jesus for us. They served us. They cooked meals for us. They arranged to have our house cleaned and walked our beagle, Toby. They sent cards. They sat with Suzy so that I could run errands. Or they ran errands for me so that I could have a few minutes of respite. The body of Christ was the source of immeasurable, unfathomable support. God was profoundly present and with us through them.

Throughout the challenges, the unknowns, and the concerns about the future, my family felt deeply loved and held close by Jesus. The primary reason for this is that each day we experienced tangible, concrete expressions of his love through our brothers and sisters in Christ. Our church family in Surrey, our church family in Missouri, and our friends scattered across the globe were, to us, the hands and feet, the mouth and words of Jesus each day. I am incapable of expressing the level of gratitude that I feel for these people. The journey would have been very lonely without them.

In some ways, it felt as if I belonged to a club that gave benefits to its members. It was a wonderful and delightful club. There were people there who brought me joy. It was a club that gave me a safe place to cry and allowed me to grow. It was a group that encouraged me, carried me, lifted my chin, and wrapped me in a deep, warm embrace. It was a group of people who, although not perfect (by any means!), nevertheless sought to point me to the cross and daily showed me Jesus. They helped me remember that he is the wholeness for which I longed. This club is called the "body of Christ." And just to think about it, just to type this paragraph, brings a flood of tears to my eyes.

God purposely intended for all of us to have this club. He knew we would face challenges and walk in darkness while we traverse life on the earth. And he gave us each other and called it his body. The church. The people of God. I don't know how anyone could face the struggles and trials of life without a caring, nurturing body—a brotherhood and sisterhood, a club—to carry him or her through.

One dear saint in Christ, a fellow member of the body, wrote a note to me during this phase of our journey that said, "You have carried us with you and your family. It is time now for us to carry all of you. We are in it for the long haul...we are in it with all of our prayers and love for as long as it takes." Those words renewed my soul and brought light in my life unlike any other moment I had known. Such hope in a short paragraph from another member in this very unique, very special club. I was reminded that God was indeed present even if I did not see him. God was tangible through the love of others.

I'm pretty sure that this is what Paul meant when he wrote, "Carry each other's burdens, and in this way you will fulfill the law of Christ" (Galatians 6:2). In fact, I think the note I received is an exact illustration, a living example of Paul's words.

The love and support were so overwhelming and touched our hearts so deeply that they gave me an entirely new understanding of the terms "Christian community," "the body of Christ," and "brothers and sisters." Their loving care modeled for me the deep, deep love and grace of Jesus. That is something I knew before. But now it has a new meaning because our Christian community made it palpable, tangible. Every single day. I found myself laughing and celebrating and dancing and mourning and grieving and weeping and wondering in a whole new way because I did those things while they were holding us and carrying us. It nourished our souls in a way I have never known before. I am deeply, profoundly grateful to those people around the world who loved us, prayed for us, cared for us, and carried us through our brain-cancer journey. Even though it felt at times as if God were distant and removed, these dear friends reminded us and showed through their actions and tangible examples of love that God was still present and always with us.

Challenges with Community

There were, however, some times when the community of support was unpredictable. I was occasionally surprised by what people did. And sometimes I was surprised by what they didn't do. A few people whom I expected to be a significant resource for help were barely present. A few people whom I would never have thought would even care or notice us became integral resources in our journey. Nevertheless, people were amazingly loving and supportive, allowing us to struggle and seek healing as they held us and loved us.

Yet for all the wonderful, encouraging, and supportive things that people did for us, there were still some moments, some occasions, when our expectations were not met. There were some unhelpful responses from a few people and even a time or two when we felt let down. One person wrote a letter to Suzy telling her that the reason she had a brain tumor was because she had not confessed her sin or asked for God's forgiveness. The letter went on to explain what this person thought Suzy's great sin was that needed to be confessed. I threw the letter in the trash and never replied. Another friend wrote to me shortly after Suzy's death and told me that he felt called by God to walk with me in the dark days that were ahead of me. He said that he wanted to meet with me regularly to allow me a safe place to vent, to share, to cry, and to struggle with my loss. I was deeply touched by his offer. But I never heard from him again, even to this day. While some people went out of their way to tangibly care for us, others made offers or promises of a visit or a meal that never materialized. I genuinely struggled in trying to figure out how to respond to the people who hurt us at a time when we were already deeply wounded.

Although it is not a profound insight, it was still significantly helpful to me when I came to understand that all of us are wounded. Each of us has been hurt, and each of us struggles, in some way, at some time in our lives. We are sinful. We are broken. We are needy. And out of our own woundedness, we hurt others, whether intentionally or accidentally. Sometimes people said the most terrible things to us even though they intended their words to be helpful. Sometimes people were impatient, uncaring, or judgmental. Each of us in our sinful brokenness has done this in some way to someone else. We are broken people, helping (or sometimes hurting) others who are also broken.

One of the most important roles that the body of Christ plays in our lives is to remind us of the grace of God in Jesus. Friends in Christ help to make his presence tangible to those on the journey who are wounded. These brothers and sisters help to remind us and to illustrate that his blood has covered our sin. He has paid the price that we owe. Our forgiveness has been purchased at a great price. We need to remind one another of this. We need to call one another to live in this truth. When we are broken and hurting, we need to encourage and remind each other that God has already provided all that we need. My brothers and sisters in Christ reminded me and urged me to focus on this truth when I struggled with being hurt by someone else.

The best response I could offer to those who hurt me was to forgive them. It wasn't easy, especially when their words or actions hurt my family. Nevertheless, God taught me through this journey that the best thing the body of Christ can do is to live as Jesus lived—to love sacrificially and to offer forgiveness. I confess that I wasn't very good at this, but I tried. I'm not sure I saw a difference in the others, but I definitely saw a difference in me. As I attempted to extend his grace to others, his grace flooded into me again and again.

God has a plan for our growth and maturity. It is with other brothers and sisters in the body of Christ who are also on the journey with us, for better or worse, that we find that maturity.

God's Purpose for Living Stones

God's desire for our lives is that we will "grow up" in him (Ephesians 4:15). While there are many things we can do to help this process, we cannot, by ourselves, create maturity. It is something that God does in us as we allow his spirit to move, to shape, and to change us. But the scriptures make it abundantly clear that we do not do this alone. In I Corinthians, Paul uses the image of a body with each part working together to form a whole (1 Corinthians 12:12ff). Peter writes of "living stones" (1 Peter 2:5) that are built into a larger, more significant and purposeful building. We are called to journey *together*, to work and live *together*, to encourage, support, challenge, and inspire maturity *together*. This is God's purpose for us.

I read a story recently about a man whose wife bought him a special guitar for his birthday. It had a unique design that was developed due to a scarcity of resources during World War I. Pieces of wood were coupled together to form the body of the guitar in place of one complete piece of wood. This design, however, produced a richer, deeper tone than other guitars that are not made in this way.

This is how God works in the community of Christians. He creates something greater, grander, and more beautiful out of pieces and fragments. He blends and combines them to make something far better than the sum of any of the pieces. In God's design, many different people from many different backgrounds, each possessing different gifts and abilities, are molded together to help each of the individuals to "grow up" as God designed. As a result, parts that are weaker, even those broken and wounded, are not only given a place in the design of the whole but actually make significant contributions to it as well. God becomes tangible, present with us, as we experience love, grace, and forgiveness in a community of believers.

Friends Helping to Make Jesus Real

When the paralytic could not get to Jesus, the man's friends creatively arranged to lower him through the roof so that Jesus could touch him (Mark 2:1–5). I imagine that it was a little scary lying on a mat that was dangling from a hole in the roof. But I know personally that there is genuine confidence in knowing that it is your friends who are holding the ropes tightly so that you can get to Jesus. And there is even greater confidence in knowing that, as the mat is lowered, you are being placed in the care of Jesus. Their efforts literally take you directly into his presence.

I imagine the man was thankful for some friends who loved him enough to carry him to Jesus. Yes, indeed. Thankful. And grateful. And humbled. Thank God that he sends friends like this into our lives to be his vital, life-giving presence in our brokenness and woundedness.

God's people working together. The body functioning as each part does its work. People growing up together, praying for, supporting, and encouraging others in the body, and bringing each person to Jesus. This is how we mature. This is how we grow up. This is how a God who seems distant is made real and present for us.

Seeing the Unseen

Of course, it is not always so simple. It is difficult and challenging to remember this. We get busy with our lives, distracted and disoriented, forgetting that God's purpose for us is to grow up, together, in him. Yet whether we are aware of it or not, God continues to shape and mold us. Sometimes we need another person in the body to help us see that. Sometimes God gives us a unique experience to show us how he is indeed powerfully present and to let us see how he is at work in the people around us. We can see God in a new way as he shows himself to us through a perspective that we had not previously seen.

Perspective is a funny thing. Two people watching the same event draw drastically different conclusions. An individual looking at his or her circumstances might see enormous challenge. Or perhaps that person sees tremendous possibility. Do we just have a bunch of lemons, or are we making lemonade? Perspective.

One day our commute to Suzy's scheduled doctor's visit at the hospital took over an hour and a half (instead of thirty-five minutes). An accident had closed a major road, and we (along with thirty-six million other drivers) had to find an alternative route. I was grumbling. Suzy said, "Isn't it nice that we are not lying by the side of the road?" Perspective. Kind of a funny thing, I guess.

The doctor's visit included routine tests and checks. Suzy's medications were constantly tweaked and adjusted. There was a lot to think about and remember. A lot of hassle. And then the nurse asked, "Can you recommend a book to help teach my children about God? My daughters are asking, and I want to make sure they learn the important things for their faith." Suddenly the visit was not a hassle or an imposition or a frustration. There was God showing his presence and purpose in everything we do in our lives. Perspective.

The scrip for Suzy's new medication was turned into the pharmacy at the cancer center. They had a reputation, and it was not for being quick or efficient. So I sat down to wait. In the hospital. Oh, how I relished that! The wait was barely tolerable in a room crowded with patients and caregivers. Once the prescription was finally ready, I went to get Suzy so we could go home. She had struck up a conversation with two women on the other side of the cancer ward. One woman told Suzy how she came to faith in Jesus through an Alpha course but that she was not currently active in a church.

Suzy was encouraging her to grow in her faith and be connected to a body of believers. "Ah, Lord, this is why you delayed us in getting here. This is why we waited, again, for meds. It's all part of your grand plan." Perspective.

Long ago, Israel was at war with the Arameans. Elisha the prophet continued to tell the king of Israel the enemy's plans as God revealed them to him. So the Aramean king sent a party to Dothan to capture Elisha. His servant awoke in the morning and saw an army of horses and chariots surrounding the city. He was worried and asked Elisha how they would ever get out of this one.

> *"Don't be afraid," the prophet answered. "Those who are with us are more than those who are with them."*
> *And Elisha prayed, "O Lord, open his eyes so he may see." Then the Lord opened the servant's eyes, and he looked and saw the hills full of horses and chariots of fire all around Elisha.*
>
> *—2 Kings 6:16–17*

God opened my eyes that day. He let me see those hidden in the hills, fighting his battles and fulfilling his purposes. He allowed me a glimpse that reminded me that when I see traffic jams and waiting rooms, I am looking at the wrong things. He showed me something I knew but perhaps had forgotten: those who are with us are more—far, far more—than those who are with them. He showed me very clearly that even though I do not always see him, he is nevertheless completely and powerfully present. Perspective.

God is present even if we do not always see him. I pray that your eyes will be opened today in a new way as God reveals to you his plans, his purposes, his truth, and his majesty. I'll be honest: it is a pretty spectacular view if you're willing to take a look.

God's purpose for believers is to keep each of us focused on his singular purpose for our lives: to become mature in our faith. He gives us the gift of others to accompany us on the journey. Occasionally he gives us a glimpse of how he is working behind the scenes. But in all of it, God's intention is that we will encourage and support others to know him, love him, serve him, and follow him as each day we become more and more like him. There is no greater thing that the church can do than to give the wounded, hurting sojourners a place of safety and respite, a place where they can be loved and reminded that God is with them, is for them, and loves them deeply. We *are* his presence, showing his love and extending his grace to one another.

Whether life feels beautiful or painful, whether we are experiencing great joy or deep crisis, God calls us to walk *together* on our journey toward becoming mature in Christ. God is indeed present with us, in our community, in spite of seeming distant.

Chapter 3

God Is Holy in Spite of the Brokenness

The second brain surgery, September 2012, and the start of end-of-life care, January–June 2013

SOMETIMES SMALL CHANGES stay small. And sometimes small changes become big changes. In the summer of 2012, a routine MRI scan revealed a change, a small spot in Suzy's brain at the site of the original tumor. The doctor warned us that this might mean that the tumor had returned. Or it might mean nothing at all. We just had to watch, and wait, to see what that "small thing" would do. Another MRI was scheduled for eight weeks later.

But the small change in Suzy's brain became a big change. Because of some challenges with speech and comprehension, she requested to have her MRI done sooner, in late August. The medical team quickly arranged for this, and we met with the neuro oncologist the next day to hear the results. He told her, "Your tumor has grown substantially." It was, in fact, larger than the first tumor they removed. Sadly, this time a small change rapidly became a big change.

The tumor board met and recommended a second brain surgery, which took place in the fall of 2012. The goal was to remove as much of the tumor as possible. We had been down this road before; we were better prepared this time, but we still scrambled to make arrangements and manage the details. There was still an emotional toll as our heads were spinning with how quickly all of this was happening.

After the surgery, Suzy received infusions of a relatively new drug, Avastin, for three months before the tumor returned again. This time it was even more ruthlessly aggressive. Suzy was losing more and more words. She could no longer read and write. The vision in her right eye was severely compromised. And the headaches had returned. It was very obvious that the tumor was back.

The options were severely limited. The few additional treatments that were possible came with substantial risks and little promise of being effective. After discussion with the team, we made the decision in early February 2013 to stop all further treatments. This was an agonizing, heartbreaking decision. As much as I wanted to do everything possible to keep fighting this tumor, we realized that a decision had to be made to stop the treatments. We entered a new phase in the brain-tumor journey. In this final phase, called "palliative care," Suzy's symptoms (headaches, seizures, loss of mobility) were addressed, but no direct treatment for the tumor was given.

Suzy was given a walker to help her move until she eventually became permanently bound to a wheelchair. Aides began to come to our home to assist with personal care. Other equipment was added as needed. My heart became weary watching the signs and signals as the tumor progressed. I also began to notice and be aware of the moments of joy that God sent into our days. I wanted to celebrate the many ways that Jesus showered grace in our lives. The grace was undeserved and unwarranted. Yet it is just his nature to pour more and more of it on us. I soon realized that there was a profound sacredness in walking that road—seeing, feeling, and tasting the signs and signals that God dwells in the interactions and exchanges of our lives. The moments and breaths of every day were made holy by the God who loved us, held us, and carried us on the road.

A Holy God

Traditional mainstream theology teaches us that God is holy, literally "set apart." God is not like the humans he created in that he is all-knowing, all-powerful, and all-present. He is without sin. He is pure and without fault. He is complete. He is whole. He is holy.

Sometimes that holiness breaks into our lives like the sudden blinding light of the sun emerging from behind a cloud. We may be surprised to see God's holiness intertwined in our own lives. We may be caught off guard. We may not even be aware of the holy moments infused with God's presence. Though we are sinful, fallen creatures, we still have experiences of God's holiness within our lives.

There were indeed some aspects of our broken journey in which God's holiness shone through powerfully. As I struggled with Suzy's decline, watching my sweet love become incapacitated, babbling and wetting herself, I decided to look for things that were good, pure, and wholesome in our pain-filled experience. One day in June 2013, in the midst of Suzy's end-of-life care phase, I wrote a list of the things that I found holy about our journey:

> We are on a sacred journey. This is a hallowed path we trod, filled with divine encounters. Holy moments:
>
>> Giggling together over the made-up word that just came from Suzy's mouth;
>>
>> Praying over Suzy when I put her to bed at night;
>>
>> Talking about what it will be like to meet Jesus face-to-face;
>>
>> Eating meals together as a family: discussing, laughing, enjoying;
>>
>> Walking into Suzy's room, praise music playing on the iPod, seeing her eyes closed and her hand lifted high above her head;
>>
>> Watching Zachary and Micah tenderly care for their mother, attending to her needs and helping her to find the words that won't come out;
>>
>> Carrying her breakfast tray to her bed then sitting down to talk through the events of the day;
>>
>> Walking with the love of your life to the moment when you have the privilege to place her in Jesus' arms.

Take off your shoes, for the place where you are standing is holy ground.

—Exodus 3:5

Indeed.

Still there were vast portions of the journey, particularly in these final months, where I struggled to find even a shred of God's holiness in any form or degree. The humiliation and loss caused by the tumor's assault on her brain were very difficult for me to absorb and understand. Suzy's loss of mobility was a challenge indeed. That was nothing, however, compared to the painful challenges caused by her decreasing ability to speak coherently. Suzy was a highly verbal person. I used to tease her that every thought that entered her mind came out of her mouth. She processed her thoughts and feelings aloud. Often. And to see her reduced to babbling incoherent phrases, frustrated because she could not form the words necessary to communicate with us, was heartbreaking.

At one point in this phase, a friend asked me, "How much of Suzy's communication are you able to understand?" I replied that before that time, I thought we were getting about 75 percent of her meaning. However, at the time he asked the question, we were probably understanding less than 50 percent of her intentions. That percentage became lower and lower until it reached the point where almost nothing she "said" was intelligible. Along with this, I was never certain that the words I did comprehend actually meant what she was trying to say. Her yes to my question did not always mean yes, nor did her request for a drink mean that she was thirsty. There were a thousand other possible meanings, and I could never be certain which one was correct.

I became increasingly discouraged by the humiliation of Suzy's condition. And I became increasingly angry as the vibrancy of the woman I loved slipped away from me.

If God is a holy God—and with all my heart I do believe that he is—then why did this part of our lives have to be so humiliating? Why did it feel so very unholy, as if God had chosen to leave us alone in this disease? Shouldn't a holy God shine through even in the brokenness of brain cancer? This all felt so dirty and mundane...and I was looking for holy!

One day I was cleaning up Suzy's incontinence for the umpteenth time. While I was doing that, God gave me one of the most powerful insights into his holiness that I have ever known. I wanted so badly to bestow on Suzy as much dignity as I could muster as the incontinence (along with everything else) caused her embarrassment, fear, pain, and confusion. This was supposed to be a sacred journey. I wanted for it to be filled with holy moments. But I found it very difficult, sometimes impossible, to catch even a glimpse of holiness in the middle of Suzy's pain, confusion, anxiety, and incontinence. Many days felt like anything other than holy.

At this stage, our days became mundane, filled with routines of bathing, dressing, looking at pictures, or sorting (again and again) through the cards sent to Suzy. More often the days felt deeply painful. It hurt me to see Suzy wince or cry in pain. It broke my heart to see her tears flow when she was confused or anxious. There was a rawness that I cannot describe as I watched this vibrant, alive, joy-filled woman go through days like this. My heart ached because every day I already missed her terribly.

Holy? Are you kidding me?

It was at this point that God reminded me that perhaps it was precisely right there, where I sat, that holiness could be discovered. "Holy" might just be found in holding a hand through anxiety or cleaning that which is dirty or picking up what has been spilled. Because holy is not, and has never been, found in pristine and perfect. Instead it shines through the messy brokenness that defines our lives.

Holiness shone brightly in a dirty, dung-strewn stable. Holiness advanced through washing dirt-caked feet. Holiness radiated from the wounds of a thorny crown and the horrendous reality of a brutal, criminal's death on a splinter-infested cross. Now that was holy. And there was nothing pretty or desirable about it. Jesus was born in a common, ordinary way. He performed the mundane duties of a servant for his band of followers. He died in a common and brutal way. His birth, his servanthood, and his death met no one's definition of perfection. Nevertheless, holiness found its truest definition in Jesus.

Should I have expected my journey to be different? Should I have thought that I would find holiness outside of the horrible path on which I was walking with Suzy? Perhaps what was wrong was not the path filled with anxiety, tears, and pain. Perhaps what was wrong was my expectation that it was supposed to be anything different than that. Perhaps that exact moment, as I cleaned up the incontinence and sought to bestow honor and dignity in Suzy's embarrassment and confusion, was what God intended as holy because it drove me to tear-filled surrender and dependence on his grace to carry me through.

Maybe what "holy" is all about is learning that nothing in this world or life will bring satisfaction. Instead we turn to the One who eases the burden and fills the void left by the assaults of the path on which we trod.

What if my greatest disappointment,
and the aching of this life,
is the revealing of a greater thirst
this world can't satisfy?

—*Laura Story, "Blessings"*

Dirty and mundane are not what I expected holiness to look like. I do not normally go looking eagerly for opportunities to give things up or to live sacrificially. But perhaps God's holiness shines most profoundly in the dirty, mundane agony of our broken lives. Wiping drool from Suzy's mouth was not my idea of a holy activity. God told me that there was very little anywhere that could be holier than doing just that.

What do you find in your life, in your own situation, that seems ordinary, mundane, or, dare I say, unholy? Perhaps this is the first place to look for God's holiness in your pain and brokenness. Because this is perhaps the point of your greatest need and deepest longing, leading you and gently nudging you to know and love and walk more closely with Jesus. And that, dear reader, is holy.

In an upside-down world, can we see God's holiness in spite of the humiliation and degradation of our shattered lives? Can we take it a step further and see God's holiness *shining through* the humiliation and degradation?

God is holy in spite of the brokenness.

An Important Word for Caregivers

If you are caring for a loved one with a terminal illness, you are walking a painful and difficult path. If there were only one thing that I could tell you, one sentence that I would want you to remember, it would be this: "You are doing a good job."

Being a caregiver is overwhelming. I was constantly filled with doubt. I second-guessed every decision and every action. I never felt certain that I was doing the right thing. And even if I felt that it was the right thing, it still very often did not feel like a good thing. The choices were often between equally difficult and painful options with a very high degree of uncertainty as to the effectiveness of any choice. Hurtful, sometimes agonizing consequences resulted from a few of the decisions I had to make. Nevertheless, I had to choose that option.

Your road is a tough one. Your loved one is dying, and you have no power to affect the outcome. Most of the time, you feel as if you are not able to do enough. Most of the time, you feel that what you are able to do is still not good enough.

You likely struggle with your own feelings as well. It is very easy to feel sorry for yourself and to wonder, *Why me?* Some caregivers feel angry. Others are intimidated by the enormity of the task. All of these feelings can then also produce feelings of guilt, even though they are normal, human reactions.

And the road is so very, very, very lonely.

I know. I walked on that road also.

So please hear this truth, dear friend. *You are doing a good job.*

You are exactly the right person to make the decisions. Your loved one may not be able to tell you how much he or she appreciates and values you, but it is true. Many of your friends and most of the people in your life can never understand or fully appreciate how very difficult this is for you. They won't be able to adequately affirm what you are doing, no matter how hard they try. You may not feel adequate for the task. You may struggle with regrets. You may think you cannot face one more day. You may feel unworthy and unloved.

But I want you to read these words, slowly and carefully. Imagine that God is expressing these very words to you. Let them echo and resonate inside of you over and over and over again. *You are doing a good job.*

Chapter 4

God Is Loving in Spite of the Pain

The final months of Suzy's life, July–September 2013

God is trustworthy in spite of the script.
God is present in spite of seeming distant.
God is holy in spite of the brokenness.

PERHAPS THE GREATEST challenge for me to accept was the fourth truth: God is loving in spite of the pain. This truth embodies and epitomizes most of all that all the world is upside down.

There were often times when I whined and complained about the changes we faced. I struggled even more as Suzy declined and deteriorated in front of my eyes. Nevertheless, there were some times along the journey when I was still able to feel and experience God loving me. In spite of the horrors we faced, at times I could somehow still acknowledge the love God was pouring over us. The experiences in this phase of the journey still haunt my memory. But

God managed to make sure that I knew, beyond all doubt, that I was loved.

The New Normal

I strongly disliked when people talked with me about "the new normal." I understood what they meant. I agree, in principle, with the concept. But I really do not like the phrase.

Over the course of these weeks (not to mention the previous months and years), we experienced many changes and adjustments. The pill boxes were bursting at the seams with all of the medicine Suzy needed. Within the span of one week, the doctor would sometimes adjust the dosages down and back up and then back down again. Some medicines were stopped and new ones started, and then the old ones would be added back in. Some pills were given simply to counter the side effects of other pills. My head swam keeping track of it. Maybe the reason I hated the phrase so much was because our new normal meant constant change.

Yet I found myself grateful—strangely enough—for these constant changes and for the adjustments that swirled around me. They reminded me every single day that I had an anchor, a rock-solid foundation that never changes. The frustrations of the changes drove me back into the arms of Jesus. And for that I am so humbly thankful. Our new normal served as a constant reminder that this world is not our home. I hungered for something that can never, ever be satisfied on this side of heaven. Our new normal illustrated that hunger each day as I was lovingly reminded that in Jesus Christ, the hunger, the longings, were already fully satisfied.

What if the changes, the new things, each day could be seen as simple reminders of God's unchanging, unceasing, undeniable love showered on each of us?

> *Yet this I call to mind and therefore I have hope:*
> *The steadfast love of the Lord never ceases,*
> *His mercies never come to an end.*
> **They are new every morning;**
> *great is your faithfulness!*
>
> —*Lamentations 3:21–23 (emphasis mine)*

In spite of the changes and challenges, there were times when God's love broke through in powerful ways. When I paused long enough to consider these times, I experienced again the truth that I am a deeply loved child of the Most High God!

Being Loved

There was, however, one thing that caused me tremendous distress: the pain. The pain was—and still is—the worst part of the journey for me. Watching Suzy hold her head or cover her eye because of the pain inside her head was an agonizing experience. When I was dressing her, at times she cried out in pain at my touch or even a gentle movement of her arm. This caused me untold distress. Although the morphine doses rose higher and higher, the neuropathic pain (damage to the nerve endings that cause them to send unusual or incorrect messages to the brain) was nevertheless excruciating. The morphine did little, if anything, to alleviate this. Suzy's pain was escalating daily, and it was an overwhelming challenge to stay proactively in front of it.

I, too, experienced a debilitating pain as I helplessly watched the love of my life slip away. Sometimes I would sing to Suzy (although this was perhaps the source of some of her pain). We had a song that was "ours": Nat King Cole's "When I Fall in Love." I would hold her hand and gently touch her arm while I sang the lyrics to her, affirming how my heart leapt in love each time it again discovered her love for me. Tears streamed down my face every time. They still do.

I thought, *How can God be loving when both of us are living with this much pain?* Surely a loving God would do something—anything—to ease Suzy's physical pain. And I wondered daily what threshold of emotional pain I could endure. I questioned, even doubted, whether God truly loved us.

So I tried to remind myself that I was loved. Even if I didn't feel it, I made a point to tell myself that God loved me. The dialogue in my head would go something like this: *At my best and my worst, God loves me. On my good days and on my bad days, I am embraced and treasured. When I perform well and when I fail miserably, I remain a loved child of the Most High God.*

But I admit that at this stage of the journey, it often felt as if there were more of the "worst," the "bad days," and the "fail miserably." Indeed, it broke my heart to see Suzy in pain and not be able to do anything. It was often frustrating beyond imagination to try to figure out what she was telling me and just not get it. When her confusion frightened her and brought tears to her eyes, my eyes overflowed as well. And I just couldn't change this. So I had to be reminded often that I was still loved, embraced, and treasured as a child of the Most High God.

That message came through to me most clearly from Suzy herself. In spite of my failings and bad days, she still loved me. She was patient with my stumblings and encouraging when I was down on myself. She still let me know that I was treasured and important. Many words failed her, but somehow she could still get out "love, love, love you" every time. And my heart melted every single time. To be loved and cherished by the person you value more than any other—well, isn't that just the message of love that God wants us to know?

Unconditional love. Agape love. It is a God kind of love. In our deepest pain and darkest nights, still there is joy in being loved, cherished, and valued. And every now and then, we have the rare privilege of experiencing it with another person.

How great is the love the Father has lavished on us,
that we should be called children of God.
And that is what we are!

—1 John 3:1

We are loved. We are loved without measure, without restrictions, and without conditions. God loves you in your brokenness and in your pain. In your loss and in your grief. In your confusion and in your worry. You are loved. That is a profound truth that we all need to ponder over and over, again and again.

I came to embrace, slowly but certainly, the simple and deeply profound truth of God's love for me. It is not conditioned on behavior. I do not receive a greater measure when I perform well or behave appropriately. I do not receive less of God's love when I fail him. I am, quite simply, loved. This simple truth gave salve to my wounded heart during the worst of the pain.

A Perspective on Pain

I've come now, however, to understand a deeper, more profound truth. I believe that *sometimes* God allows us to be hurt in order to heal us. Sometimes God allows the pain as an act of his love. By no means do I intend to imply that all grief, pain, and brokenness in the world are God's actions. Sometimes we feel pain as a direct result of sin, and sometimes we feel pain because we live in a sinful and broken world. But *sometimes* God allows us to be hurt so that we can be more completely healed.

Some days—a very few days—my faith was strong, and I felt confident that God was working all things for good and that I could trust his plan even when I didn't see it. But some days—most days— I wept. I was angry. I shook my head, and, on occasion, I shook my fist as well. I did not understand why God continued to allow Suzy to be in pain. I ached for the vibrant, alive person she once was, who, at that point, was reduced to babbling and wetting herself. And I wept tears upon tears. Even though she was still alive, I missed her so greatly, so deeply that it physically hurt inside. Then I would hold her hand, clean her up, whisper that I loved her, and melt into more tears at seeing her beaming smile and her crooked, misshaped mouth that labored to form the whispered words "love you."

The tears. The tears. The weeping and crying. The tears. What is Jesus doing when there are so many tears?

Good theology—in Jesus and in us—coexists with broken hearts, shattered lives, and unimaginable pain. It produces a reservoir of patience toward ourselves and others who hurt and cannot understand what is happening. Jesus not only gives Mary space and time to sorrow deeply; he sorrows with her.

—*Carolyn Custis James,* When Life and Beliefs Collide

Jesus wept with Mary and Martha not because of the death of Lazarus. Jesus knew what was about to happen. He wept instead, I think, because of his love for them. He knew that God's sovereign, wise, powerful plan sometimes brings pain and tears to those he loves. The plan is still perfect. God is still omnipotent. But for a time, a short time or a long time, the finite creatures feel pain, loss, and degradation. And they weep. So out of deep, deep love, he weeps with us.

When Zachary and Micah were young, I took them to the doctor for their immunizations. They cried when they were given the shots. I cried with them. Even though I knew that what was happening was ultimately good, I still wept tears for their pain. And even though I was the one who took them in for the shots, they nevertheless curled up in my arms and buried their heads in my chest, knowing they were loved and would be comforted. More tears flowed then as well.

A few weeks before Suzy died, I wrote these words:

Today I sit, weeping in pain, curled up in my Father's lap, knowing that he loves and comforts me. Even though it is his plan that has brought us to this, I have nowhere else to turn. Instead of rejecting me, laughing at me, humiliating me, or discarding me, he holds me tight, and he weeps. He weeps for me. He weeps with me.

He knows Suzy's pain, and he knows her loss. And he weeps for her too.

We want for love to be pretty and joy-filled. We like the fantasy of believing that love is a good feeling. We are deceived when we assume that if an experience is difficult or challenging or even painful, then it is not loving. That is simply not true, and the perpetuation of that falsehood causes even greater pain.

Sometimes love is painful. Sometimes it hurts. But it is still love. When Zachary and Micah were given their immunizations, they likely questioned why I allowed them to be hurt. Yet I don't think they questioned my love for them in spite of the pain. As children, they could never understand that the pain was for a much greater good. They knew that even with the pain the only place to turn was to the one who loved them most, even though I allowed the pain.

After the tragedy of September 11, 2001, Queen Elizabeth said in a speech that "grief is the price of love." We would feel no pain, no grief, and no loss if we felt no love. And given that choice, I will choose to feel love every time, even when it is painful. In your painful situation, in the challenges and overwhelming circumstances that surround your life, can you pause and consider the deep love God has for you? Perhaps you are experiencing a temporary pain, or perhaps your brokenness is a long-term, life-altering, never-ending challenge. My encouragement is that we remember that God's love is never capricious, never temporary, never random, and never built on our response to it.

Your pain may be from your own sinful choices, or you may be the victim of someone else's sinful choice. Or there may not be any possible reason that you can discern for the pain. In a world of randomness and unreliability, the one true and trustworthy thing we have is this: God loves us. He proved that love when he sent Jesus to die on a cross so that we would always know, forever and ever, that we are loved.

In the upside-down life that we live, can we understand and embrace the truth that God is loving in spite of the pain?

Suzy's Final Weeks

In the final weeks, we continued walking on our painful, hellish journey. Suzy continued to slowly decline, and I saw less and less of her every day. Her body had been cruelly assaulted. Her mind and her personality likewise had taken hard, direct hits from the tumor. I was stunned every time I saw her smile, and my heart melted when she managed to whisper, "Love, love."

Most GBM patients deteriorate and die very quickly. But our path was slow and torturous. I tried each day to be thankful for additional time with Suzy and the privilege to hold her hand and give her a kiss. Yet I also struggled mightily with my emotions, watching the love of my life fade, seeing her in physical pain and humiliated by the degradation that her tumor caused. I often had to explain very simple things to her. I frequently stopped her from putting something into her mouth. Yes, each day was a gift, but there was also horrendous pain in accepting that gift.

Psalm 42 became my friend. I wept through the verses, struggling each day to "put my hope in God, for I shall yet praise him." In honesty I admit that some days (maybe most days) I didn't feel at all like doing that. Nevertheless I tried to choose hope, trusting that God knew and understood what I did not.

At this point I felt that my faith was holding on by a thin, fraying thread. Ironically, my greatest strength came in holding on to Suzy's faith. While mine was weak, hers remained robust. She loved Jesus and could not wait to see him face-to-face. I marveled at her faith, and I always loved her grace-filled way of living. She was always the most vibrant, Christ-reflecting person I knew. I hope that someday I can hold even a fraction of the confidence and trust she exhibited daily. Her vibrant faith inspired and encouraged me to continue trusting the one to whom we had committed our lives.

Each day of these final weeks brought Suzy closer to her greatest joy and highest aspiration—to be with Jesus. She was ready to meet him. She was eager to be in his arms. She had no fear and no worries. She simply trusted. I was trying to take each day, each moment, to care for her and shower love over her until I had the privilege to place her in his arms.

As the days wore on, I witnessed with anguish Suzy's pain increasing ever more. Her appetite decreased, and in the final weeks, she ate very little. She slept most of the time. Just six weeks before she died, she was sleeping sixteen or eighteen hours each day/night.

This increased to twenty or twenty-two hours every day in the two weeks leading to her death.

I sat with Suzy during the brief times when she was awake. We looked at cards that friends had sent. I told her stories about our life together: special vacations, funny things that Zachary and Micah had done, ministries to which we had given our lives. We listened to praise music together. Sometimes I sang to her the songs from our wedding or other songs we have appreciated through the years. Although she could communicate little, she responded to my questions and thoughts with a smile, a weak nod, and, rarely, a whispered response.

I felt an enormous sadness and grief for her pain and confusion. It seemed as if she was confused about most everything. When she was sitting in her wheelchair, she would lean down and fiddle with the left wheel and frequently turned her body while trying to look at something that was behind her. Despite constant reassurance, she was often upset thinking that she was supposed to do something or be somewhere. She worried and even panicked over this. I struggled daily with the humiliation and degradation this tumor brought to her life. I felt sadness also knowing that for a while we would be separated. I continue to hold on tightly to the truth that one day we will be together again, healed and made whole, with an eternity to laugh, to dance, and to be together as we worship and adore Jesus.

In the final week of her life, she did not get out of the bed. Her right arm and leg had ceased to be usable months earlier, and her hand and foot curled in cruelly, causing strong neuropathic pain. Her eyes worked independently from one another, so focusing was nearly impossible. Her field of vision was severely limited, and trying to focus or concentrate on anything only made her headaches worse. The left side of her head became grossly misshaped with a deep indentation at her temple and significant swelling around her cheek and jaw. I reached a point where I was not sure what threshold of this hell I could endure. It was horrendous to watch helplessly as the sweet love of my life lingered in pain, degradation, and humiliation caused by a mass growing inside her brain.

I cried every day, often several times a day. There were so many, many tears. One of my favorite quotes collected during my journey is this:

> *There is a sacredness in tears.*
> *They are not the mark of weakness, but of power.*
> *They speak more eloquently than ten thousand tongues.*
> *They are the messengers of overwhelming grief…and of unspeakable love.*

> —*Washington Irving*

In her final days, she ate no more than a few bites of food along with drinking a few sips of apple juice. When she was awake in bed, she pulled at her covers and picked at the catheter bag around her leg. She mumbled incoherent words and sounds but, on occasion, still managed "thank" and "love." She was most content to just be with me while I held her hand.

The aides who came to care for Suzy cleaned her up and helped with fresh clothing and sheets. They loved her and tenderly attended to her needs. She was a favorite among the many clients they cared for, and they often asked their supervisor to be scheduled to be with her. The doctor, who visited daily, marveled over how Suzy continued to defy all medical understanding of the progression of GBM. The nurses, who also came daily, commented on Suzy's pleasant demeanor. In her final days, she refused oral medications and therefore had to be given daily injections. After pushing meds through a needle into her stomach, they could not believe when she said, "Thank."

I know of no person anywhere at any time who has lived his or her life with the grace and joy with which Suzy lived hers. I cannot imagine any person better able to exude dignity in spite of the horrendous assaults of her disease. Throughout her life, she bestowed honor on each person she was with and continued with an uncanny ability to make you feel as if you were the most important person in the world.

In the second century, Irenaeus wrote, "The glory of God is man fully alive." Suzy has always been the most fully alive person I have ever known. God was deeply glorified in her living. And it was clear that he was also deeply glorified in her dying. In spite of the fact that the pain was excruciating and the hellish journey felt unending, right in the middle of it all, Suzy was fully alive. Fully, completely, unashamedly, abundantly alive. In life *and in death*: fully alive.

Notes Written during Suzy's Final Days

September 12, 2013

It has been a very long good-bye. I've sought diligently to say what is important. I've tried to live in the moment and embrace the extra time we were given, no matter how painful those long days were. I wanted my good-bye to be honoring to God. And I've prayed every single day that I could communicate to Suzy in way that she was certain that she was loved, cherished, and adored.

Suzy will very soon be dancing in fields of grace, held and embraced in the arms of Jesus. I watch and wait for her final earthly breath and subsequent birth into a new, free, whole, glorious life. I weep tears of joy and tears of grief, all mixed together, and I'm not sure I can distinguish them one from another. What a strange paradox for one's heart to ache with overwhelming pain and leap with joy and gladness at the same moment.

September 15, 2013
Suzy sleeps. I wait.
Suzy sleeps. I weep.
Suzy sleeps. I yearn and long for peace.
Suzy sleeps. I pray.
Suzy sleeps.

Suzy stirs. My heart flutters.
Suzy whispers a few mumbled sounds. I reply, "I love you, love you, love you."
Suzy sighs. I squeeze her hand and sing to her, "When I fall in love, it will be forever…"
Suzy settles, and her breathing becomes slow and deep again.
Suzy sleeps.
Suzy sleeps.

I will lie down and sleep in peace,
for you alone, O Lord,
will keep me safe.

—*Psalm 4:8*

September 17, 2013
I have fought the good fight.
I have finished the race.
I have kept the faith.

—*2 Timothy 4:7*

This morning at 8:45, Jesus called to Suzy, "Come home, my precious daughter." She took her last breath on earth and flew into the arms of Jesus. It was peaceful and gentle and, oh, so holy! Now she is dancing, praising, and worshiping the God to whom she has devoted her whole life. Her fight is done; her race is over. Her faith is complete. She is healed. She is whole. She is radiant. She is fully alive!

III

Making Sense Out of Upside Down

My journey through the initial months of grief,
September–December 2013

God is trustworthy in spite of the script.
God is present in spite of seeming distant.
God is holy in spite of the humiliation.
God is loving in spite of the pain.
Upside down. Backward.

If buttercups buzzed after the bee,
If boats were on land, churches on sea,
If ponies rode men, and if grass ate the cows,
And if cats should be chased into holes by the mouse,
If summer were spring, and the other way 'round,
Then all the world would be upside down.

I HAVE CERTAINLY known upside down. My life was uprooted, turned over, turned inside out, and, indeed, turned upside down. It has been painful. It has been lonely. It is a journey I never wanted. It is a life of which I never dreamed.

No one told me that grief would hurt so deeply. Not just emotionally. For me there was an actual physical pain in my stomach that remained for months, reminding me daily of my loss and brokenness. Even when I had brief moments of happiness at seeing an old friend or enjoying family time, the dull ache in my stomach constantly reminded me that all was not well. Pain became a constant, unwanted companion.

Yet in spite of it all, these four affirmations remained true: God is good in spite of the script. God is present in spite of seeming distant. God is holy in spite of the humiliation. God is loving in spite of the pain. That is all so very upside down and backward. How on earth could I ever make sense of a world, a life, a journey that was so completely upside down?

Learning How to Walk (Again)

I'm fascinated with the moving walkways at airports. I wonder why anyone would just stand (on the right, please) when they allow you to walk (on the left) and cover ground much more quickly. But there is that little moment, that little stutter step, at the end of the moving walkway. As the voice from nowhere warns you, "Watch your step," you take a step off, your body moving a little more quickly than your feet are ready for. For just half a second, you catch your balance and reorient to a new pace of walking. *This is what my grief felt like.*

In the first months after Suzy's death, I felt hopelessly trapped in that half second. I felt as if I were endlessly trying to find balance, forever wondering what it means and looks like to reorient. I felt as if I were learning to walk again.

For the six months before Suzy's death, I was consumed with her care. Everything around me halted as I devoted myself to her. Suddenly I had to learn how to walk again as I reoriented my life to a more familiar pace. On a larger scale as well, I struggled greatly in facing what life would look like without Suzy. We were married for almost twenty-six years. I admit that those early steps were painful and horrible as I stumbled along, trying to take new steps. I could not find my balance, and reorientation seemed hopeless. I was trapped in that half second.

One morning, my counselor told me, "You are in completely unfamiliar territory, and it seems scary to you." (Oh, boy, did he nail that one!) It reminded me of a scene in C. S. Lewis's book *The Lion, The Witch and the Wardrobe*. Lucy discovers the lion Aslan, the God figure. She asks if he is safe.

"Safe?" said Mr. Beaver. "Don't you hear what Mrs. Beaver tells you? Who said anything about safe? 'Course he isn't safe. But he's good. He's the king, I tell you."

Those stutter steps and falls, that disorientation and feeling like I was lost, all made me feel very unsafe. Indeed, Barry, watch your step! And I have to be honest and tell you that God did not feel very safe to me at that time either. But I held on to the truth that Mr. Beaver makes clear: "But he's good."

I carefully watched my step in that very unsafe half second, waiting for God to take my hand and lead me on new paths. I didn't know what it would look like. I didn't know when the world would begin to make sense. I often wondered if there was a limit to the number of tears one human can shed or a depth of pain that a heart can no longer bear. In those first weeks and months after Suzy died, everything felt very, very unsafe. But I held on with every fiber of my being; even when I wasn't sure that I could hold on anymore, I clung to the truth that God is good. "He's the king, I tell you." And in my mind, that had to enough as I learned to walk again. It had to be.

Those early months of grief forced me to continually review and relive all the memories of those painful months when Suzy deteriorated and eventually died. That year, 2013, will always be remembered by me as a year of painful, hellish waiting, longing, and loss. It was a year of tears upon tears upon tears. A year of deep loneliness. A year of agony. And the numbers 2-0-1-3 will always remind me of the year that Suzy, the sweet, sweet love of my life, breathed her last. We said good-bye to the most vibrant, loving, vivacious person I have ever known. We buried her cremains. I closed accounts and started to adapt and adjust to life as a widower.

Yet, in my grief, I came to realize that there were definitely some parts of 2013 that were good, even wonderful. We were loved beyond measure by our church family and by friends all over the world. We experienced God's grace in the hardest, most challenging circumstances. Even at my lowest points, I still felt held. Always. God showed up in ways I had never before imagined. And although I never want to walk through anything like 2013 again, I can say that I have known and experienced God's love in deeper and more profound ways than I ever dreamed could exist. And of greatest joy to me is the truth that in 2013 Suzy was fully healed and made whole, no longer suffering and no longer in pain. She is in the arms of her truest and deepest love, worshiping and adoring the Savior that she spent a lifetime telling others about. I will always remember that 2013 was the year of Suzy's full and final redemption, when she received the reward of eternity and the privilege to dance arm in arm with Jesus. I am confident that she is radiating joy and that her huge, infectious smile is lighting up every corner of heaven. It was Suzy's year for completing her faith and finishing her race.

But, oh! How I miss her!

"My Grace Is Sufficient..."

There is much in our lives as followers of Christ that is backward. Our faith is often viewed as upside down when those outside of it look at us. The kingdom of God is, in truth, radically upside down. We are told to love our enemies. We are commanded to bless those who persecute us (Romans 12:14). We are called to deny ourselves (Luke 9:23). It seems profoundly backward to welcome the idea that "He who wants to be great must be a servant" (Matthew 20:26) and that the only way to find your life is to lose it (Matthew 10:39). Jesus told us, "For even the Son of Man did not come to be served but to serve" (Matthew 20:28). Our faith can seem upside down and backward.

How do we make sense out of this? How do we understand God's goodness in spite of a terrible script? How do we welcome God's presence when it feels that he is so distant? How do we embrace God's holiness and love when the path we trod is broken and painful? How do we live our lives when our faith seems upside down and backward?

The apostle Paul knew about pain. He experienced brokenness. Although we cannot know with certainty the exact source of that pain and brokenness, Paul tells us in his letters about a "thorn in his flesh" (2 Corinthians 12:7). He repeatedly and urgently pled with God to take it away. He talked to a God who is good and trustworthy, who is present, who is holy and loving, begging to be released and relieved of the pain and brokenness of this "thorn." He received no relief. He only received God's answer: "My grace is sufficient for you, *my power is made perfect in your weakness*" (2 Corinthians 12:9, (emphasis mine).

That is an upside-down, backward reply. And it is the foundational truth that will carry us in our own pain and brokenness.

This is the way in which God works. It is where God's most profound and life-changing work occurs in our lives. It is his sufficient grace in our weakness, pain, and brokenness that matters in all things. This is the perfect way that God designed it. It is the perfect way that "upside down" actually makes sense.

We do not have the privilege of deciding and defining what "good" means as the scripts of our lives unfold. It is not in our power to make the call regarding what "holy" and "loving" should look like. God does. And although our finite and limited human minds may struggle mightily to understand and make sense of it, we nevertheless live every day under the sovereign and all-encompassing reign of God, who is trustworthy, present, holy, and loving by *his* terms and *his* definitions. And when we don't understand, when it all seems backward and upside down to us, God does not chide or reprimand us. He simply tells us, "That is OK. My grace will make up for what is lacking. My power is working better and more strongly in the places you think it is not present."

What is more, while it is tempting to focus on our own pain and brokenness, it is essential that we remember the pain, the loss, the suffering, the humiliation, and the degradation that Jesus underwent *on our behalf*. In the cross of Christ we are forgiven. The blood of Jesus makes us whole people. Through the cross we are given a gift that we could never earn or merit: the gift of eternal life. This comes from a God who is trustworthy, who is present, and who is holy and loving. A God who gives this free gift called "grace." And he tells us—he tells you, and he tells me—"My grace...it is sufficient. It is enough. It is all that you need."

It may look and feel backward. We may think it is completely upside down. We may argue with it, rebel against it, or fight it off. We may not embrace or welcome it. It is given freely, fully, and completely nevertheless. It is right. It is true. It is sufficient. It is enough. It is complete.

Because of the cross, I am certain that today Suzy is completely whole. On September 17, 2013, she was completely healed of the tumor that cruelly assaulted her brain. I celebrate that she now knows and experiences complete and total joy. I "see" her talking and laughing and worshiping face-to-face with God. And if she could, I think that she would tell us how very good and trustworthy, how very present, how very holy, and how very loving God is. In spite of the script and seeming distant, in spite of the brokenness, and in spite of the pain, he is trustworthy, present, holy, and loving. And he proved that at the cross.

What Should I Say? How to Care for Those Who Are Grieving

We are meant to be the tangible hands and feet of Jesus to those who are wounded. We are asked to give words of encouragement, to pray with and for, and to extend grace to those who are struggling. A person who is in the midst of a life-altering illness or in deep grief over the loss of a loved one needs to know, to be reminded, that God is present in spite of the fact that he seems distant and that he loves that person in spite of his or her pain. This is our calling.

But what should a person say? How do we do this? How can one offer God's healing presence and extend his grace when he or she is worried about saying something that will make it worse? Imagine for a moment what a wounded, grieving person would say to you about the fact that you desire to help but you don't know what to say.

"Please, invite me to join you for lunch. Ask me to meet you for coffee. Include me in your plans for a Saturday afternoon with friends. Ask me to go for a walk with you or to get a drink together. Even if I say no, please keep asking. Please keep asking me for a long, long time. Don't let my no turn you away. I need you to stick with me. Please."

A person in grief needs ongoing support and care for a very long time. In the pain of Suzy's illness, during her deterioration, and for long after her death, I desperately needed people. I needed them (and I still do need them) to love me, to care for me, and to encourage me. I needed them to pursue me and not wait for me to make the first move. I needed them to talk about Suzy, to tell me memories of good times or funny things she said. I needed them to bring her name up in conversations. I needed them to stick with me even when I didn't feel like I was worth it. I needed them to keep doing this for months, even years.

Sadly, most people immediately join in grieving a loss and then move on with their lives. But the ones left behind—the spouse, the parent, the child—will grieve for far longer than everyone else. Some people were uncomfortable with my grief. Others urged me to "get over it" and "move on." Others pretended as if everything was all right even when my world was falling apart all around me. But there were some who understood, who got it. They stuck with me (and still do) for the long haul. They love and care. They patiently listen without giving advice. They ask how I'm doing and really want to know. They share stories and memories of Suzy with me. They are the hands and feet of Jesus to me.

This is desperately needed. The Christian community should be the first place where it is safe for people to grieve and mourn the loss of a loved one, no matter how long it takes. The community should be the place of the deepest love and encouragement, support, and care for those who have experienced loss. Because Christian community is the place where Jesus' love is made tangible. It is the most important source of healing comfort that God tangibly provides to us. Yet many in the Christian community pass too quickly on the opportunities to share in this kind of love.

Some people have told me that they "just don't know what to say." I think that many are afraid that they will make things worse if they talk with me, asking about my grief. Or they fear I will dissolve into tears if they mention Suzy's name to me. Please know this important truth: you cannot make things worse by talking with a person in pain and grief! Such people are already hurting; they are already low. You won't create more difficulty by entering into their lives in a loving and supportive way. It is wonderfully encouraging to know that someone else cares, that another person is thinking of us and wants to help. Even if someone does cry when you mention a memory or say his or her loved one's name, this is not a bad thing. Those tears are an important part of the healing process. Your tender, gentle, patient care and presence are likely the very things that are needed. Don't hold it back; instead offer it freely—even if the person says no again and again.

Many people told me that they were at a loss for words. What do we say to the one who is grieving? I have said numerous times that the most significant thing that you can say is, "I'm sorry for your loss. I loved her too. I miss her too." This validates my feelings and tells me that you share in my loss with me. These words, which can be spoken in various ways, help the one grieving know that he or she is not alone and that others are on the journey with him or her. If you did not personally know the person who died, ask the one grieving to tell you about him or her. Those in grief have a very high need to talk about their loved ones. Yet most people do not have enough patience to listen. So ask them to share stories and memories. Ask them about birthdays and holidays. Ask them about special vacations or other shared experiences. Ask them what they need and how they are doing. If they don't want to answer now, ask them again later. Again and again. Please, just don't give up on them!

I loved receiving and reading the cards and letters that people sent to me. Those that shared a special memory of Suzy were particularly cherished. I saved all of them and still read through them from time to time. You can write to your friend or family member who is grieving and share these kinds of stories as well. They are wonderfully healing for a grieving soul. The world in which we live allows us to stay in touch electronically, via e-mail or Facebook. We can call the person on the phone. We can call a person anywhere in the world via Skype or other Internet applications. These letters, notes, cards, e-mails, messages, and calls can continue for many years. The grieving person will deeply appreciate your attentive care and shared memories. He or she will need this for a long, long time.

IV

Mosaics of Redemption

The beginning pictures of God's redemption in my life, 2014–present

IN THE PREFACE to this book, I shared the following quote:

> *When suffering shatters the carefully kept vase that is our lives, God stoops to pick up the pieces. But he doesn't put them back together as a restoration project patterned after our former selves. Instead, He sifts through the rubble and selects some of the shards as raw material for another project—a mosaic that tells the story of redemption.*

> —*Ken Gire,* Windows of the Soul

Of all that I read and pondered during the three and a half years of Suzy's illness and in the time since her death, nothing has spoken so profoundly, penetrated so deeply, cut so painfully, and healed so graciously as these words.

The first lesson that I struggled to embrace was to simply accept this truth. As my family journeyed through our daily lives, turned upside down by a brain tumor, I was certain that God was picking up the pieces of the shattered vase. I felt him doing it. I saw him doing it. I sensed and experienced it. But I was equally certain that God would put it all back together the way it was, the way that I wanted it to be. Instead, throughout the three and a half years and in the years following, there has been a slow and often painful awareness of the fact that God was creating something new. Some of the shards that he chose to use were ones I wanted to leave behind. I fought and rebelled at times, challenging God to make something worthwhile out of the ugly, broken bits of the shattered vase. But slowly, painfully I came to accept that God was designing something new, even beautiful, with the brokenness of our lives.

There is, however, a second, and I think more important, lesson. In many ways I am still learning this truth. I have come to see that there is something more than just accepting the truth of God's rebuilding project. And that something more is for me to not only accept it…but to embrace it. To welcome it. To walk in trust, looking expectantly, dare I say even eagerly, to the new thing that God is building in my life. For most of the journey through Suzy's illness and my grief following, I would never have been able to say this. However, I have come to a new awareness, a new understanding by which I can state that I find joy, contentment…peace in welcoming God's building project. Learning to embrace this, to welcome this, is the most profound and significant thing that has happened in my entire life.

God is making something beautiful out of the sharp, jagged, ugly shards of our broken vase. A new mosaic is taking shape, one that tells, in a new way, a story of redemption. And for that truth I am not sad or sorry. Of course, I miss the old vase. There are many smiles in remembering the days of joy and celebration that the old vase represented. And although I do not feel those same feelings today, there is still a peaceful contentment in knowing that, while far from completed, this new building project, this redemption-bearing mosaic, brings joy and contentment in ways I never imagined possible.

With humility and gratitude for God's designing work in my life, I share with you some of the lessons that God is teaching me and the mosaics that he is creating out of my brokenness.

CHAPTER 5

God Is Teaching Me...

OUR JOURNEY THROUGH the challenges of Suzy's brain tumor lasted three and a half years. Along the way there were countless lessons learned. Most of them are still being learned by me. These are one aspect of God's redemptive mosaics in my life. I share with you here some of those lessons. Following are a collection of items that I wrote at various times reflecting on the lessons God is teaching me. Some are reflections on scripture in the light of the experiences in which we found ourselves. Others are lessons on various themes. I pray that you can see the new mosaics that God was (and is) creating in my life through these lessons. Part of the new mosaic he is making is for my life to increasingly reflect the values of these lessons.

God Is Teaching Me...to Trust His Promises
You try to see what is inside. You look through the window. It is blocked, and so you see...nothing.

You look in the mirror. You hope for a glimpse. It is so cloudy that you see...nothing.

You ponder tomorrow, or next week, or this summer. You try to make plans. But it is all uncertain. And you see...nothing.

I have struggled greatly in learning to live faithfully when every ounce of control was ripped from my hands. This is not easy for anyone; it is especially challenging for those of us who have a type A personality. God is clearly teaching me to trust.

So when everything is cloudy, unclear, uncertain...is there anything certain, anything dependable, anything I can lean on? Anything at all that I can truly trust?

Jesus Christ is the same yesterday and today and forever.

—Hebrews 13:8

Know therefore that the Lord your God is God; he is the faithful God, keeping his covenant of love to a thousand generations of those who love him and keep his commands.

—Deuteronomy 7:9

Your love, O Lord, reaches to the heavens, your faithfulness to the skies.

—Psalm 36:5

There are many other promises in scripture. All of them remind me of the same thing: God is faithful. He always has been. He always will be. That certainty will carry me through a cloudy, unclear tomorrow, a tomorrow that I do not yet see. That certainty will sustain me next week and next month. I cannot depend on anything else—because there is nothing else on which to depend. With every fiber of my being, I believe and trust that God will be faithful.

But I confess to you that I still struggle at times with believing completely, with believing to a point that I can place all my trust in God, not relying on my own strength. Yet I'm slowly growing in my ability to trust a faithful God. He is the one true certainty in a maddening, upside-down, chaotic, swirling, messy world.

God Is Teaching Me…to Embrace Waiting

Little did I know it at the time, but our journey was the beginning of a very long period of waiting. Through all of it there was much of my life that was in a holding pattern while I waited on God. I often rebelled against waiting. Sometimes I shouted and shook my fist, demanding to have answers and direction immediately. Still I waited. And slowly, surprisingly—sometimes painfully—something happened. While I waited, God was at work in me. Waiting became an important avenue through which God wanted to form me into a new creature.

The answers to the challenges of our lives are not always simple or obvious. There are times when we are required to wait before we can receive the results of a test. Job applicants are often informed that a decision may not be made for weeks; they are left waiting to discover the answers as to their applications. A host issues party invitations and then waits for each person to respond. No reason to buy groceries or plan seating until all those invited have responded. Just wait.

Perhaps the most challenging aspect of waiting for answers is when we ask God for direction but do not yet have a clear sense of his answer. We want to know which college to attend or what to do about a certain problem that has been bothering us. We ask God. Then we wait.

I've often thought there must be a more efficient way of getting answers from God. Surely there must be a simpler way to give me direction or help me with a decision. Waiting and wondering cannot be the most efficient or effective ways for humans to discern God's will in their lives. Yet this is most often the method God chooses. While we wait for answers, he is busy with something, only revealing the answer when he knows that we are ready or when the situation warrants our action.

What is it about our world, about our lives, that makes us think that we can achieve without waiting? What messages, subtle or overt, have we received that indicated we somehow deserve to have what we want without waiting? I wonder what happened in my life that made me dislike waiting so intensely. Do I really believe that I deserve to have answers, results, direction before they are ready?

Christians actually know a great deal about waiting. It is inherent in our faith. God is not the God of quick fixes or just-add-water instant spiritual growth. Walking with God toward spiritual maturity takes an entire lifetime, not one day less. Our whole lives are spent waiting for God's transforming work to be completed in us. We are also in the ultimate waiting game as we look for, long for, anticipate, and eagerly expect Jesus to return. It may be today. It may be tomorrow. It may be a thousand years from now. We don't know. But we will wait, trusting that God has everything perfectly planned and completely under control.

Be patient, then, brothers, until the Lord's coming. See how the farmer waits for the land to yield its valuable crop and how patient he is for the autumn and spring rains. You too, be patient and stand firm, because the Lord's coming is near.

—*James 5:7–8*

Sometimes waiting can be so aggravating! But sometimes there is an incredible joy in it as we consider the event for which we wait. We look ahead and feel excitement over the anticipated event even though it has not yet arrived. I tried with every ounce of my faith to look forward to Suzy's physical healing from the tumor. I certainly look forward to Jesus' return. And I realize the only thing I can do is wait. I pray, "*Now*, Lord, please, now."

Even so, I found contentment in knowing that he was holding me, calming me, comforting me. I may not like to wait. But I certainly welcomed his healing love and nourishing grace that was poured over me while I waited.

Waiting for answers creates anxiety. We may wonder if we missed something or were unaware of God's direction. We think that other people are moving forward with clarity so we should be also. The pressure, whether self-imposed or placed on us by others, to know the answer can be overtly intense. The resulting anxiety can literally make us ill. It might manifest physical symptoms that make the waiting even worse.

So consider this startling truth: Whether it involves answers to our questions or results of our blood tests, waiting is the normal medium through which we will receive that for which we look. We will not receive our answers magically, through the wave of our hands or the snap of our fingers. The answers cannot be produced by wishing (or praying) harder. The normal route to receive that for which we look is…waiting.

But while I waited, God began to reveal himself to me in new ways. He worked on some of the rough edges of my character (there are plenty) and molded me, little by little, to be a bit less like me and a bit more like Jesus. He used me to encourage other people and allowed me to see things that I would have otherwise missed. When you sit and wait, you have time that was never before available to see God's hand at work and his will slowly revealed before your eyes. In the midst of waiting, I felt held by God. Held. I sensed his presence in the middle of a dry and barren wilderness. There have been overwhelming experiences of discovering that even if I do not have the answers or know the future plan, I am nevertheless still loved, cherished, and valued. I am reminded again that I am a precious child of the Most High God.

And all of this happened while I was waiting.

God Is Teaching Me…to Live with an Undivided Heart

One morning after Suzy's second surgery, I drove through heavy traffic to visit her at the hospital. As I drove, I was praying. I asked God to help me grow and know him better with an undivided heart. I am painfully aware of the distractions that lure me away and try to capture even a small corner of my heart. I was reflecting on that issue as I drove. Oh, that we would live each day with an undivided heart of commitment. God is growing each of us toward this purpose, friends.

The hospital did nothing to help with my divided heart. Hospitals are filled with distractions. Noises, busyness, people bustling everywhere. It is hard to focus, hard to even think clearly. How can a patient get better with so many distractions? And so I wondered, *How much of my life is filled with such distractions, noise, busyness, and bustling?* Sadly, I think my life is significantly filled with that. God in his graciousness brings peace in the busyness and quiet in the noise. "Be still and know that I am God" (Psalm 46:10) is not so much a command as it is a promise. He is not telling us we must do this; he is reminding us that he does this for us. I pray for stillness and quiet to truly know you, God. I pray for your peace and rest, stillness and quiet. It is the hope of this great promise that sustains me.

God Is Teaching Me...to Believe That He Is Leading Me Daily

When Suzy was first diagnosed, I learned some very hard (and sometimes painful) lessons. God wanted me to trust him. God wanted me to believe that he was leading us every single day—even when I was not sure that I wanted to trust in that. As we progressed through Suzy's treatments and tumor recurrence, I found that this simple lesson was still being taught. On every step of our brain-tumor journey, it was a matter of choosing confident trust and belief that God was leading us.

What does it look like to walk in trust? What does it mean to let God lead you daily? Can I live and breathe and carry on each day trusting that God is good? Do I trust that where he is leading me and how he is working are for my good and his glory? How has the journey with Suzy's brain tumor shaped my faith?

I remember one event that happened during the period without tumor progression. The nurse oncologist called me with the results of Suzy's MRI. "It all looks good. There is nothing of significance to report or worry about." I paused and offered a prayer of thanks and praise to God. Most certainly God is good. Most assuredly I praised and honored him for this great news.

But that event set me to thinking: Would I have reacted differently if the news were different? Would I have said thank you to God if the nurse had told me that the MRI showed that the tumor was back? Would I have praised him so boldly and confidently if we found ourselves on that day dealing with recurrent glioblastoma as we did later in our journey? Are my faith and trust shown differently in response to good news than to bad news?

I stopped to ponder these truths that I had always said that I believed: God is always good. God is always loving and gracious. God is holy and pure, strong and wise, powerful, pure, and perfect. Always. Those truths do not change when our circumstances change. They are true whether the sun is shining or the rain is pouring down. You can always count on them whether the path is clean and clear or dark and murky. God is God when the scan is clear and when it is not. These are truths that even today I am still learning to trust. I am continuing to learn that I can believe with confidence that God is leading me daily, whether I receive good news or bad.

During the brain-tumor journey, I came to realize how very much I focus on circumstances and situations. I am overwhelmed with how much my faith rises or falls with the changes around me. My mood and emotions sadly often overshadow my faith. It pains me to admit that. But for much of the journey, I looked at and evaluated life through the lens of my personal experiences. If everything in my life was going well, then my faith was robust. If things were tough or challenging or unclear, then I found myself struggling to trust that God is good. And that is not a faith with which I am pleased.

But my faith and trust slowly changed over the three and a half years we walked through our challenges. It changed dramatically. God stretched, prodded, and shaped me through the journey. I have learned to look at him and not at circumstances, to see truth and not situations. I have come to understand how big God is and how loving and wise he is. And I can say that I trust Him—wholehearted, complete, and total trust no matter the circumstances. If the nurse called today with news that a scan was not good, I like to think that I would still offer a prayer of thanks and praise. Because I am confidently certain that God would be there to hold me, carry me, guide me, and love me every single step of the way through whatever challenge I faced. God hasn't changed! Let the circumstances be what they are. I am choosing to keep my eyes focused on the only One who can ever truly be trusted. Our hearts will know pain and bitterness if we focus on the circumstances. Our hearts will know joy and peace when we look at Jesus and not at the circumstances.

I still have a long way to go on this journey. I still have much to learn, and my faith still needs to grow. I'm more at peace with the need to grow now than I was before because I know that I can trust God to lead me as we journey together. I still have bad days, and I still struggle, and I'm still selfish and sinful. But I trust that God is making me into a new creation. I trust that it's not about me but wholly about him. And he is always good.

You will keep in perfect peace those whose minds are steadfast,
because they trust in you.
Trust in the Lord forever,
for the Lord, the Lord, is the Rock eternal.

—*Isaiah 26:3–4*

God Is Teaching Me...to See Every Moment as an Opportunity to Advance the Kingdom

Be very careful, then, how you live—not as unwise but as wise,
making the most of every opportunity.

—*Ephesians 5:15–16*

When Suzy was in the hospital recovering from her second brain surgery, God gave us the privilege one afternoon to spend some time with Jeffrey, another patient on the ward. He was also struggling with various neuro deficits. It was a "chance" encounter, but he asked us if we would share about our hope in Jesus and our trust in God's providence. Suzy shared some verses from 2 Corinthians with him, and then she prayed for him. We always believed that God wanted to use Suzy's brain tumor to further his kingdom. What a joy and privilege to see that in a specific, tangible way in our encounter with Jeffrey.

Suzy also seized the hours spent receiving treatments as opportunities to share her faith. I remember one hospital visit when she shared her faith with two nurses and two patients in the same treatment room. She asked each one if they knew that they were loved by God and that he was in full control of their lives. She shared her confidence that Jesus was with her and at work in her body and brain. She encouraged them to look for the ways that God was already at work in them.

I have never known or seen anyone who so ardently lived each day following the exhortation of Ephesians 5:15–16. While I was busy asking questions and fretting over the answers I did not know, Suzy instead made the most of every opportunity, wisely talking about the only thing that really matters.

On another day of treatment at the hospital, we were encouraged by another person's faith. One of the other patients in the room was an older woman named Eileen. She had been in cancer treatment for fourteen years and gladly shared about her faith in Christ, saying, "A lot has to do with the Lord. Me and him has a good relationship." She introduced us to her daughter Ocean. They both agreed that God was their strength, the one carrying them through their journey. As they left, I thanked God for the encouragement we received as they also made the most of the opportunity to proclaim Jesus with us.

In a classroom, with your coworker, as you walk the dog, at the grocery, on the sideline or in the bleachers at the game, on a business trip, at a fundraiser, studying with your friends, doing chores, cooking dinner, while exercising—may each of us see the potential in the moment God has placed before us. May we be wise and make the most of every opportunity. It is not about having answers to every question. Instead it is about the moment that God has ordained for you this day.

God Is Teaching Me...to Walk on the Path He Lays Out for Me

"You're just on a different path now."

In the end-of-life care phase, as Suzy lingered so long in pain and confusion, defying the odds of survival for her type of tumor, the hospice doctor visited one day. The team, including that doctor, the GP, the district nurse, and several therapists, did an excellent job of caring for Suzy. She needed increasing medication for her pain. They also tried to address her anxiety and some minor panic attacks as her confusion increased.

As we asked questions and discussed Suzy's care with the doctor that day, I asked the question that was most frequently on my mind those days: "What is going on?"

I had pondered that question often. Glioblastomas are very aggressive, highly malignant tumors. They grow rapidly. At one point Suzy did experience a very rapid decline over several weeks. This was textbook typical of the effect GBM can have on a body. But then the decline slowed. The trend was still downward but much more slowly.

So I asked, "What is going on? Is the tumor still growing? Or..."

The doctor replied, "You're just on a different path now. You were on one path with a very rapid decline. It is what we see most often with this type of tumor. But for some reason it changed, and you are on a different path. It leads to the same place, but this one has other dynamics, other characteristics to look for and plan for."

I wasn't surprised. I knew we were on a different path. That seemed obvious. But before I could ask why, she preempted me. "We don't know why. It just changes sometimes for some patients. It has some advantages but brings a new set of challenges and concerns for you to deal with. And to be honest, she can switch back to the other path suddenly as well. We just don't know."

As a result of this conversation, I spent a great deal of time thinking about these paths and Suzy's change from one to the other. I was thankful for the additional time, the days to celebrate and appreciate the gift of life that the new path offered. But I also admit that I struggled with the challenges of this new path: lingering days with increased pain, confusion, and anxiety. I cannot say that one path was better and one worse. They were just different. And at that time, we were on a different path. For a while.

I've also done some thinking since that encounter about times in my life when I have changed paths. There have been times when I was on the wrong path, and God, in his grace, gently brought me to his path. There have been times when I had to choose between two paths leading to different places and outcomes but both potentially good and godly. I've recalled major life events—graduations, the births of Zachary and Micah, our move to England, the diagnosis of a brain tumor—when our paths changed suddenly, drastically, and dramatically. I've wondered how many times in my life I could say, "I'm just on a different path now." I know with certainty that God has used the paths—and the people, events, and circumstances on them—to shape me to be the man I am today. And I find myself filled with gratitude for the paths, even the difficult ones on which I didn't want to walk. Nonetheless, I still feel thanksgiving that there have been times when God has put me on a different path.

At this point in the journey, Suzy's ability to communicate was nearly nonexistent. I tried to imagine what she would say in response to this. I know that of greatest importance, of highest value to her, would be that every person knows that God loves him or her and desires that he or she walk on the narrow path with him, living a life of abundant joy in relationship with Jesus.

> *Enter through the narrow gate. For wide is the gate and broad is the road that leads to destruction, and many enter through it. But small is the gate and narrow the path that leads to life, and only a few find it.*
>
> *—Matthew 7:13–14*

A different path—a narrow path. Few may find it, but all are welcome and invited to walk it. The way to walk on this path is by surrendering your heart, allowing Jesus to be your forgiver and leader. It is a different path on which walking is indeed worthwhile.

God Is Teaching Me...to See Circumstances through His Eyes

> *Though the fig tree does not bud*
> *and there are no grapes on the vines,*
> *though the olive crop fails*
> *and the fields produce no food,*
> *though there are no sheep in the pen*

and no cattle in the stalls,
yet I will rejoice in the Lord,
I will be joyful in God my Savior.
The Sovereign Lord is my strength.
He makes my feet like the feet of a deer,
he enables me to tread on the heights.

—*Habakkuk 3:17–19*

It is so easy to let my circumstances dictate my mood. On sunny days, with pleasant people around me, I'm happy. But if there's no place to park in the rain or I have to deal with my mobile-phone service provider, I find myself turning angry and surly. So add to that the frustration of not understanding what Suzy wanted to say or the heartache of watching as she struggled with pain, and I found myself anywhere but in my happy place.

Circumstances. They are what they are. But are they the dictators of my mood? Are they the determiners of my reaction and response to God?

Habakkuk spent a great deal of time looking at the circumstances around him. The evildoers were flourishing. The enemy was about to invade. And he talked with God, telling him that he needed to correct the situation—now. It is not until the very end of the book, the final verses, that Habakkuk states his trust in God regardless of the circumstances. It is a lesson I have learned and am still learning throughout my journey. When I looked at our circumstances, I lost heart—there were no buds on the fig tree, no crops and no livestock; Suzy's muscles were wasted and useless, and there was incontinence and pain. I became discouraged and downtrodden. It is only when I looked at God—and I mean fully at God—that the circumstances faded so that what really mattered could shine.

As I continue in my life, I am choosing to place my trust in God—in good circumstances and bad. My only hope is to place my trust fully in the One who made me, knows me best, and still loves me even when I no longer deserve to be loved. I am still working on this. I can be distracted quite easily by the circumstances around me. But trust is a choice, and I am learning, slowly, to put full-stock trust in God. The circumstances look significantly different when you do that.

Suzy often amazed me with the trust she displayed. Every single day she found herself trusting aides to bathe and dress her, medical folks and therapists to manage meds and equipment, and me to remember how to keep track of and manage all of it. She remained the most pleasant, most cheerful, most Jesus-reflecting person I know. Her trust was firmly established. The assaults of a brain tumor, which were countless, fierce, and relentless, did not trouble her. She trusted. She had learned to not look at circumstances but at Christ. The withering fig blossoms and lack of sheep in the pen did not concern her because she believed with Habakkuk that "the Sovereign Lord is my strength."

Oh, to have the faith and strength, the courage, the wisdom, the willingness to trust, no matter the circumstances and storms that blow all around me.

One more thing: God tells Habakkuk that the enemy, the destroyer, will be destroyed (ch. 2). I take great hope in that. Make no mistake, just as Babylon was eventually destroyed, *there will be a day in our world where cancer reigns in evil terror no more.* Glioblastoma multiform will be defeated, and no one, absolutely no one, will suffer or struggle with the hell in which we walked. Until then, I will continue to unashamedly affirm my faith and trust in a good and loving God, who, at the right time, will make all things new.

Circumstances be damned. You do not win in the end. So I'm lining up my trust in the One who does.

CHAPTER 6

New Designs for My Life

I am Not the Same, and God Uses That

EARLY IN MY grief after Suzy's death, I received a card from a dear friend. She wrote, "How painful to watch her die and how ridiculously cruel to miss her now." That description—"ridiculously cruel"—had been a powerful descriptor of my life for five years, from the first diagnosis up to the present. At least that is what I thought and felt most of the time. In reality there was much for which to be thankful. There was joy, and there were new starts. But I often found myself wallowing in the "ridiculously cruel" parts on which my mind seemed to dwell. And there were many parts of all of this—the diagnosis, the illness, her decline, her brokenness, her pain, her death, and my grief—that are indeed ridiculously cruel when seen in the light of my expectations for life.

But the primary questions that I have had to ask myself are these: Do the challenges and frustrations, which still linger today, describe me or define me? Am I in this now, for now, but moving in a new direction? Or is my life now defined by the words "ridiculously cruel"? My responses to those questions determine the trajectory of my life. Do I embrace and welcome the new mosaics God is creating, or do I deny them, longing instead for a different place and time to which I can never return? *This has been the hardest work of grief in my life.*

I look back, trying to remember who I was and what I was like *before* February 8, 2010 (the day we received the diagnosis of Suzy's brain tumor). There are some parts that I can barely remember and others that I don't want to remember. But I know with absolute certainty that I am not the same today as I was then. I have changed. I have adjusted and rearranged. I have learned. I have grown. I have, dare I say, matured. God shaped and molded me through Suzy's illness. He used my grief to shape and mold me further. I am a new and different man. I believe that God uses these changes for the next chapters of my life. He intends for me to continue to grow as I walk and live and use the things that he taught me.

Holding Things Loosely

I am a list maker. Obsessively. Yes, I am one of those who even writes on the list something that I have already done, just to feel the joy of crossing it off. There is enormous satisfaction in actually seeing all you have accomplished on a list with every item crossed off.

But there are some things that cannot be completed. Not today. Not tomorrow. Not next week either. There are some things over which I have no control. Adjustments are made, and I adapt as necessary. But no matter how hard I try (and, believe me, I have tried pretty hard), I cannot eliminate them. I could not heal Suzy's tumor.

I could not eliminate the effects of the treatment. I was powerless to do anything about her slow and painful decline at the end. I wanted to do these things. I put them on my to-do list. But they just stayed there, day after day. I wanted to cross them off. But I couldn't.

For a period of our lives, we were forced to live in the in-between. We were not where we once were. We were not yet to the place where we were going. We were in between. It was a very difficult place to be for someone who likes to know a set list of things that need to be done.

Yet there were some good parts about living in between. I saw some amazing beauty there. God was using those unfinished things on the list to remind me that I needed to depend on him and not on myself. I liked that. God was showing me that his power is made perfect in my weakness. I learned things about myself that I didn't know before. I had some amazing insights.

Instead of finishing lists, our journey taught me to lean into the unknown and to walk in territory that I had not known before. I learned to embrace the journey instead of always worrying about the final destination. I learned to be OK with the unfinished and started to welcome the beauty and joy I discovered while dwelling in the in-between place. And daily I marveled at how I felt held in God's big, strong, loving hands. There are some things you will never know, some beauty you will never see, some joy you can never experience until you are in a place where the only thing to do is to sit and wait. I still don't like it very much. I'm not very good at it. But I have to tell you that there is a sweetness in knowing Jesus this way that I had never experienced before.

I don't want to check that off the list. I want it to go on and on. So as weird and uncomfortable as it feels, I am now choosing to linger in the in-between places of my life. If you care to join me, I welcome you here. Not much gets checked off the list while you are here. But there are joyful surprises while you wait. I promise you that.

Bold Faith

Sometimes I could embrace the new things God was doing with my life. But often I struggled to even see the changes. One usually can only see changes of this nature in retrospect, looking back. Other times I knew that changes were occurring, but I did not want to welcome or acknowledge them. Still, there were some times when the changes simply involved seeing my experience through the eyes of another. An unnamed woman helped me to see the changes (and potential changes) God was working in my life.

> *A large crowd followed and pressed around Jesus. And a woman was there who had been subject to bleeding for twelve years. She had suffered a great deal under the care of many doctors and had spent all she had, yet instead of getting better she grew worse. When she heard about Jesus, she came up behind him in the crowd and touched his cloak, because she thought, "If I just touch his clothes, I will be healed." Immediately her bleeding stopped and she felt in her body that she was freed from her suffering.*

> —*Mark 5:24–29*

I have enormous admiration and respect for this unnamed woman. She demonstrates the following:

> *Perseverance*: She suffered for twelve years, and yet she continued to pursue healing. Even when the odds were against her, she kept persevering.
>
> *Boldness*: In the first century, a woman had no right to touch a man. Yet she knew there was something different about Jesus. She knew what he could do. And she laid aside conventional wisdom so that she could be close to him.
>
> *Faith*. "If I just touch his clothes, I will be healed." That is confidence. Supreme confidence. Trusting confidence. I have enormous admiration and respect for this unnamed woman.

Just one of those three characteristics would make a difference in my life. Just growing in perseverance or boldness or faith would make me very happy. But the combination of all three is powerful. She demonstrates for me the kind of life—persevering, bold, faithful—for which I long. A life that is blessed. Jesus affirms, "Daughter, your faith has healed you. Go in peace and be freed from your suffering" (v. 34).

I wonder what she told her grandchildren. I wonder what she wrote in her journal about that experience. I wonder who else came looking for Jesus because of this woman's testimony. I wonder how many lives were changed forever by witnessing the perseverance, the boldness, and the faith of this woman. This unnamed, unclean (bleeding) woman. She impacted my life. And I am sure she has impacted many, many others.

Her perseverance helped me keep going when I felt like giving up. Her boldness empowered me to seek big things from God. Her faith encouraged me to hold on to Jesus, knowing that if I just reach out to touch him, I have all that I need.

I didn't want the script that was being written for our lives. I learned, however, to accept and embrace God's goodness in spite of that script as I wrote earlier. Part of God's goodness, though, was in making me into a new creature. His grace allows us to keep living in spite of overwhelming pain. Indeed, his grace *calls* us to keep living. The picture he is painting is different than before. He is making a new mosaic out of the broken shards of the shattered vase. It is a different kind of beautiful than I dreamed or imagined. Yet it is indeed beautiful because the artist is creating new creatures out of the old ones.

In your life, in your pain, and in your brokenness, I encourage you to welcome the new mosaics that God is designing. He is using the pain to shape something new and beautiful in you. It does not look like it did before. It cannot look like it did before. But it can be beautiful in a new way as God shapes and molds your character to be more like Jesus every day.

I Won't Ever Forget, but I Will Live

I was watching a television show about the lives and careers of a group of doctors in a hospital. The show portrays not only the medical cases they address but also the soap-opera kind of lives they live. All of their relationships intertwine in a magnificent, knotted mess. In one particular episode, two of the doctors were commiserating regarding the losses in their lives, their loves, and their relationships. One asked the other, "Do you think we have used up all our 'happy'?"

The question hit me firmly, striking at the deepest core of my fears. I wonder and worry about the same thing. Have I used up all my "happy"? Will I ever be happy again? Will I ever feel normal again? Will life ever bring me joy, contentment, even fulfillment? Or am I destined to wander along for the rest of my days, lost, broken, and alone because I've used up all my "happy"?

There is a way to learn to live again and to find happiness in our lives. It will not look the same as it did before. But it is still there. The key is to embrace the new mosaics God is making out of the broken pieces of our lives. I had a good life, a wonderful life, a joy-filled life before our brain-tumor journey. I will never go back to that life. Not ever. And there is a grief not only in the loss of Suzy but also in the loss of the joy-filled life we lived and shared.

But I can, I will, I do feel happy again. Not in the same way. Not as I imagined or expected it. But in embracing the new mosaics that God is creating, there is a new joy. Not like the old joy but a joy nevertheless. As long as I hold on to wanting to have my old life back, I don't think that I will ever feel joy. In that case, I have, in fact, used up all my "happy." But in welcoming and embracing the new mosaics that God is creating out of the broken shards of the old life, I can, I will, I do begin to feel happy again. And it brings a joy all its own when I welcome that.

I admit, however, that it has been very difficult for me at times to even want to feel happy. There is an irrational voice of fear that tells me, "If you start acting happy, it means that you have forgotten

Suzy." Combatting that voice has been an enormous challenge in my grief. I know logically that it is not rational. But my heart cannot always accept that truth. I want to honor Suzy's memory, to keep it alive. So I feel like I have to hold on to every aspect of happiness from my past because to feel a new "happy" is somehow dishonoring to Suzy. But I also know that she wanted me to continue living, to thrive and to flourish. I have struggled greatly with the challenges of this dilemma.

How do I now learn to live and feel happy? How do I embrace the new future God is creating for me? Does this mean I have to completely let go of the past? Do I have to forget the past in order to start to live and feel happy again? How do I strike the balance needed to make my life work with the new mosaics that God is designing while still remembering and celebrating the past?

I will never forget. I can never forget my sweet love, the radiant, vivacious, fully alive woman with whom I walked for twenty-eight years. She will always be precious to me. I am a more patient, more reasonable, more caring, more loving man because of knowing and loving her. I see her influence in many areas of my life. I see her face, hear her laugh, and recognize her loving heart in the lives of our sons. The most rational truth is that I will never, ever forget this. I will never, ever forget her.

But I will live again. I will move forward. It will not look like the dream I once dreamed. It will not be the way I hoped it would be. But it will be good if I follow the path God has laid out before me. I will live, I will dream, I will feel joy, and I will be happy in a new and different way as I welcome God's mosaics of redemption unfolding in my life.

I am still discovering the next chapter of my life. God has given me a new calling in a new land. I have entered life on a new continent. I am now teaching English (EFL) in North Africa. This was a dream that Suzy and I shared for many years, and I am finding a new joy in discovering the richness of God's plan for this phase of my life.

There are still some aspects of my future, however, that remain unclear. I wait, sometimes patiently and sometimes not so patiently, to discover how God intends for me to live as a widower and a single parent of young adults. I ache with longing for Suzy to be a part of this phase of my life. I can never forget her. But in spite of the new challenges, I am learning to live again.

Early in my grief, I wrote the following e-mail to a good friend:

> *I am hanging in there. Definitely good days and hard days, or more like good moments and hard moments. I just miss her so much—I want to discuss things with her, show her things, ask her opinion. She is not here for any of it. I rejoice and celebrate that she is healed, and I know she is having a way better time than I am right now. But sometimes it is just hard to get through the day holding on to that perspective. I try to remember it, but sometimes the tears and sadness just roll in anyway. In the good moments, I get reminders of the joy we shared, of the joy that is hers today and the joy that will one day be mine as well. I'm just moving forward very slowly.*

An amputee can physically heal from the loss of a leg but must still learn how to walk again. Just like that, I am learning how to walk again, how to walk in a new way, how to listen for God's leading and to accept that "happy" will just be different for me now.

I will never forget. But I will live.

V

Future Mosaics Still in the Making

My STORY IS not yet finished.

I've learned some incredible lessons so far on the journey. Sometimes the lessons were painful; other times they were rewarding. I have learned (and I am still learning) that, in an upside-down world,

*God is trustworthy in spite of the script;
*God is present in spite of seeming distant;
*God is holy in spite of the brokenness;
*God is loving in spite of the pain.

I've learned that "God works all things together for good" (Romans 8:28). Above all else, I've come to know the profound and foundational truth that God spoke to Paul, giving a message to all of us as well: "My grace is sufficient for you" (2 Corinthians 12:9). Always, in every way, at all times, and in all circumstances, God's grace has been more than enough. I trust wholeheartedly that it always will be.

My story is not yet finished.

I've embraced the truth that God has stooped down to pick up the broken pieces and shards of our shattered vase and has used them for a new design, for a new creation. He is creating a mosaic of redemption out of the torn, broken, ugly shards. And the mosaic is beautiful. It is breathtaking. It is precious. But it is not yet completed.

My story is not yet finished.

I have hope that God will continue to create, mold, shape, and design the broken and fragmented pieces of my life into new redemptive mosaics. I've seen him do it before. It gives me great hope that it will continue in the future. I believe that God is always doing "new things" (Isaiah 43:19), and in every way he is "making all things new" (Revelation 21:5). I am convinced that God still has plans for me and still wants to send joy into my life.

My story is not yet finished.

Are we open to the new designs, the new mosaics, that God is creating out of the broken pieces of our lives? Are we not only open to his work, but do we also, in truth, welcome this work? It can be incredibly difficult to let go of broken dreams when painful realizations bombard us with the truth that our lives are not what we planned or dreamed or hoped for. Nevertheless, God can and will bring beautiful new mosaics if we but step back and allow him to design the way he chooses. There are still redemptive mosaics to be made. I am eager to wait and watch and see what they may be!

My story is not yet finished.

Throughout the highs and lows of our journey with brain cancer, one song in particular resonated in and through my pain and brokenness as a calming salve for my weary heart. Matt Redman's "Never Once" became the anthem of my life, and I returned to its words of affirmation again and again:

Scars and struggles on the way,
but with joy our hearts can say,
Never once did we ever walk alone.
Never once did you leave us on our own.
You are faithful, God, you are faithful!

In the end, that is all that has ever mattered. The story, although not yet finished, is not my story. It is God's story. The story is not about me. I am not the central character, the scriptwriter, or the director. This is God's story. God is the author and the director. In each of our own stories, we all play minor roles and only in relationship to the main character, Jesus. And in this singular story—the redemptive story of God's grace worked out in various ways in all of our lives—there is a foundational truth: never once, never even for a single moment, do we walk alone. He is faithfully with us, loving, holding, and carrying us. He is faithfully picking up the remnants of the shattered vase and making a mosaic of redemption. He is faithful. This is the truest story of our lives.

My story is not yet finished. There are more mosaics to come. But they will be created under God's careful direction, and my life will be shaped by his faithful presence. The story will continue until the day he comes to take me to heaven. Only on that day will my story be finished. He will wipe the tears from my eyes (Rev. 21:4) and take me to a place where there is no pain or brokenness, no brain tumors, no grieving, no sadness, and no loss. He will complete my story. The redemptive mosaic will then be finished. And it will be beautiful!

31231778R00065

Made in the USA
Middletown, DE
23 April 2016